The Church Is in a Stew

The Church Is in a Stew

Developing Multicongregational Churches

by
Jerry Appleby
with Glen Van Dyne

Foreword by
C. Peter Wagner

Beacon Hill Press of Kansas City
Kansas City, Missouri

Copyright 1990
by Beacon Hill Press of Kansas City

ISBN: 083-411-3570

Printed in the
United States of America

Cover: Crandall Vail

10   9   8   7   6   5   4   3   2   1 (1990)

Contents

87560

Foreword

The alarm clock has gone off!

Pastors and church leaders, wake up!

The book you have in your hands is a terribly important document for the church in the U.S. More than any other previous book, it will help us wake up to the real social world that we Americans live in. Most pastors in America preach that the gospel must move from Jerusalem to Judea to Samaria and to the uttermost parts of the earth today as it did in the first century. But few have more than a skin-deep understanding of what that implies for themselves and their churches.

Jerry Appleby's understanding is much more than skin-deep. It has moved profoundly through his fertile mind and into his heart. He has a clear picture of what American society really is at the end of the 20th century, and his heart beats with the heart of God, not willing that any of them should perish.

As you read *The Church Is in a Stew,* you will absorb much of this knowledge, vision, and compassion. You will understand the growing multiethnic nature of U.S. society in general and your city or neighborhood in particular. You will learn not only to recognize but also to appreciate people who are different from you and yours. More importantly, you will begin to believe that many more men and women from America's minority groups can be won to Christ than are presently being won.

My personal touch with thousands of U.S. pastors across denominational lines has led me to believe that large numbers of them would like to relate more effectively to those belonging to other sociocultural groups in their communities, but they can't because they simply don't know how. This book will tell you how to do it.

The how-to focuses on the multicongregational model, that is, one local church embracing several different ethnic congregations. This is not the only way to do it, as Jerry Appleby clearly points out. But it is one of the most feasible ways for an Anglo church located in a mixed community to reach out to those around them with the love of Jesus. This book is so practical that it deals with issues such as, Which pastor gets which office? Who chooses the flowers for the sanctuary? Do we share musical instruments? How do we divide secretarial help? What translation facilities do we provide? And scores of other sensitive questions that are much better answered sooner than later.

This book, fortunately, comes not from a theoretician but from a hands-on practitioner. As the pastor of Bresee Avenue Church of the Nazarene in Pasadena, Calif., Jerry Appleby leads a multicongregational church himself, embracing Armenian, Hispanic, Arabic, and Anglo congregations. But his experience is not limited to his own church, since he is in constant demand as an ethnic ministries consultant nationwide. The concrete models toward the end of the book understandably are from the Church of the Nazarene, Appleby's own denomination. However, this is not to be seen as a book written for Nazarenes. It is a book written for and directly applicable to the entire Body of Christ in America, regardless of denominational labels.

And it is a good book. It is the best on the subject currently available. I will require it for my students at Fuller. I can't require it for you, but I can give it my highest recommendation.

C. PETER WAGNER
Fuller Theological Seminary
Pasadena, Calif.

Introduction

In a previous book, *Missions Have Come Home to America,* Jerry Appleby dealt with the reality of increasing diversity of ethnicity in the United States and Canada because of the tremendous influx of new immigrants. In this book he grapples with the more difficult question of what the Church's response to this mission opportunity should be.

To ignore what is happening within our borders is not an option.

At worst, we have to deliberately try to run away from reality by fleeing to the suburbs and in some cases by trying to find a wilderness hideaway where we can live in isolation and let the rest of the world go by. Such a stance is not practically possible, let alone Christian—unless, of course, one believes the age of monks and monasteries was the golden age of the Church of Jesus Christ.

Speaking from personal experience, I must tell you that even in the wilderness the reality of cultural diversity and the need for unity is not lessened but on the contrary is heightened.

For 8 years our family lived in a wilderness community in Alaska. For the 10 years prior, we had lived in southern California, specifically in the Los Angeles area. If we had any illusions that moving away from the metropolitan area into an isolated village located on an island and accessible only by air and water would bring release from either cultural tensions or dependence on others, we quickly abandoned such notions.

When someone in our wilderness village was in trouble

or lost or overdue on a fishing trip, we didn't stop to ask his cultural viewpoints or his social status. We just joined hands and resources in an all-out effort to find, rescue, or help him. A basic survival instinct took over, and we became a community in action to rescue a fellow human being.

The world is chiefly inhabited by other people. And sooner or later (usually sooner than later) we are going to have to interface with them for our own survival and growth.

But even more important, we are called on as followers of Jesus to pour out our lives as He did in love for our fellowman. So rather than seeking isolation and independence, Christians are called on to put themselves in a position where they are vulnerable to all the variety of peoples with which God has populated the world and to find a way to live together harmoniously to His glory.

It has been my personal privilege to have crossed and paralleled paths with Jerry Appleby on a number of occasions. The Pacific area, especially Hawaii, was our first baptism into multicultural ministries. Moving out of the comparatively stable environment of the Midwest in the 1960s and 70s to serve the church in the middle of the ocean was a positive, hands-on experience for us both.

In the early 1980s we both worked for Dr. Raymond W. Hurn, a pioneer in the area of ethnic ministries, church planting, and church growth. This gave us a continent-wide view of the rapidly developing multicultural challenge facing the Church in North America.

Once again, in southern California through the Los Angeles Thrust to the Cities, we have been forced to wrestle with the problems facing the Church in a major city where culturally changing communities are forcing local churches to either find solutions or attempt to move into some "wilderness isolation" mode.

I am honored to share in the preparation of this book

with Jerry. Working alongside this fellow practitioner has been one of the most rewarding experiences of my ministry.

The title of this book has a double meaning. First, the Church, if it is really the Church, is a stewpot and not a melting pot. It is a place where people of differing educational, financial, social, and cultural backgrounds come together around a common belief in Jesus Christ.

The Church is indeed in a stew. The very atmosphere in which the modern Church in the United States and Canada exists is like a seething caldron into which all kinds of people are being dropped.

So, one way or another, the Church is in a stew. It can be a positive experience, as in a recognition of the beauty and flavor to be enjoyed when cultural diversity is accepted and blended with spiritual unity; or it can put the local church in a stew about what to do if it tries to deny the reality of the world that is forming around it.

All the ingredients are available to the Church for making an attractive dish that can be served to a world starving for love and acceptance. What is needed are some chefs (pastors and churches) willing to work out some nourishing recipes.

Please pass the stew!

GLEN L. VAN DYNE

The Purpose of This Book

The call of the Church to go into all the world is a call to cross boundaries of language, culture, and customs that normally divide us from each other. Christianity is above culture. Yet, from the first Christian century, every local manifestation of the Church of Jesus Christ has existed in this present world in a specific cultural setting.

As the Church has grown geographically and matured in its outlook, it has come to the realization that it is time for cultural barriers to come down and in their place to emerge a spirit and practice of mutual understanding and learning from each other. This, of course, is easier said than done.

Human nature (a factor in the Church, too, in case you hadn't noticed) is prone to keep us all snugly locked inside our own ethnocentric cocoons. Such a position is no longer practical, let alone acceptable (if it ever was). You are invited to have a part in breaking the church free from such limitations as we explore in these pages the concept of the multi-congregational church in a multicultural community.

This is a very simple "how-to" book. It is the writers' prayer that it will be used to bring a better understanding of cross-cultural dynamics and their relationship to the local church's efforts to reach out to the multicultural communities surrounding us in increasing numbers.

You could be reading this book for one of at least three reasons:

1. You are about to start a cross-cultural ministry in your church for the first time, and you are wondering if what you

know about the Church, Christian doctrine, the Bible, and interpersonal relationships is sufficient to effectively communicate the gospel to the different languages and cultures in which your church is situated. This book contains insights that can enhance your effectiveness as they are applied to your own situation. The viewpoints offered can serve to sharpen your thinking and action as you go along.

2. Your church has already started a ministry to other ethnic groups. Perhaps your experience has allowed you to travel or even live overseas. Now you are curious to see if what you have already learned about differences between your own culture and other cultures and starting churches cross-culturally is confirmed in these pages. Broad exposure to differing cultures is valuable, but there are bound to be surprises and new lessons to be learned when you set out to make cross-cultural ministry a reality in your local setting.

3. At the present, your church is not participating in a cross-cultural ministry. But for some time this has been a need in your neighborhood. You have enough savvy to realize that there is some specialization that will be required to meet that need. You have looked at or heard of the multicongregations now in existence and feel that this is the answer to the needs of your church. You are hoping this book will start you off on the right track, giving you knowledge to minister effectively with all the people groups of your neighborhood. Hopefully this book will help you avoid some wrong turns as you begin the exciting journey into the land of multicongregational reality.

Many books deal with the task of reaching the cities of today. Others deal with communicating cross-culturally. The specialty of this book is describing a method of church planting allowing for the uniqueness of each culture to be balanced with the mandate of the Scriptures to unity. The large influx of people into the major cities of the world means most of these efforts will be concentrated in urban areas.

It is written with one reader in mind. This book is specifically for the pastor and Christian worker in multiethnic neighborhoods.

It covers more than one approach. Each chapter is designed to give guidelines that can be used in various cross-cultural situations. However, it is careful to recognize that the organizational and administrative approach may be different according to the section of the country or the culture(s) confronted.

It is short and basic. This book is written with a plain fact of church life in mind: Pastors and church leaders are extremely busy. If you're typical, you're already overburdened with "required reading." The last thing you want to do is wade through page after page of text to get to a bottom line of advice. This is not a scholarly book. It is designed not as a book of mere wishful thinking but rather as a practical book for those needing some direction.

This volume will help you do the job. It is not the last word on the subject. If you desire to do further research, there are other books available to assist you. However, the insights, tips, and guidelines to come will give you a definite edge over those of us who began works without a guide.

It is easily read. The general approach to this book is to have a basic, easy-to-follow outline. This will allow you to drop into a chapter at your interest level and drop out as you desire. You do not have to read every word to get helpful suggestions for your situation.

In cross-cultural church work, no one, no matter how impressive his credentials, can be the final authority. Cross-cultural trainers, language experts, authors, editors, pastors, laymen, and a host of others have contributed directly and indirectly to what is found here. You will be wise to engage in the same kind of personal research as you become a multicongregational leader.

With this in mind, we invite you to look at a church model that may be the answer to reaching your neighborhood for Christ.

JERRY APPLEBY

Definitions

Many intercultural and multicultural terms reflect recent developments and therefore have a variety of definitions. This is common when new concepts are discussed. There is nothing new about intercultural or multicultural human relations, but by combining these with communication, culture, society, education, and psychology, a difference emerges that may create some confusion. Defining certain key terms may be helpful.

Basic Terms

Culture—the customs, beliefs, and characteristics of a particular group, whether racial, religious, or social. This includes all ways of living: values, beliefs, aesthetic standards, linguistic expressions, patterns of thinking, behavioral norms, and styles of communication that a group of people have developed to assure their survival in a specific physical and social environment.

Subculture—a group of people within a larger cultural group who share enough linguistic or dialectical characteristics to distinguish them from others in the same society.

Race—a group of people with more or less the same distinctive combinations of hereditary physical characteristics. This is not necessarily interchangeable with the terms *ethnic* or *culture.*

Class—a group of people within a society who share basic economic, political, or cultural characteristics. Examples might include: wealth or its absence, kind of labor performed, family background, linguistic characteristics, or sets of special attitudes and behaviors.

Ethnic Group—a group of people identified by racial, national, or cultural characteristics. Ethnic group membership is normally determined by birth. The term *ethnic group* is often applied to groups considered to have a minority status (whether numerical, class, or culture) in the larger society.

Language—a systematic, structured, verbal, and, in most cases, written code used for communication among a group of people. Language and culture are determining factors in the way people think, the way they communicate, and the way they behave.

Dialect—a variety of a spoken language that differs from the standard form of the language and is used by a group of speakers who are set off from others geographically or socially.

Communication—the transmission of messages from a sender to a receiver in any one of a variety of codes, i.e., language, gestures, signs, written symbols, etc.

Prejudice—hostile and unreasonable feelings, opinions, or attitudes based on fear, mistrust, ignorance, misinformation, or a combination thereof, and directed against a racial, religious, national, or other cultural group.

Multicultural Terminology

Cross-cultural—interaction between two or more different cultures.

Multicultural—the existing and functioning of more than one culture. In a sense, most people have lived or worked with other cultures and thus are multicultural. This in no way implies that it is a positive or a negative experience.

Cultural Pluralism—refers to the cultural diversity within a given political or social structure. Many people, for example, are replacing the melting pot theory concerning American society with the idea of cultural pluralism. This recognizes the multiethnic and multicultural contributions of the American way while encouraging the maintenance and development of different life-styles, languages, and convictions. Equally important is a commitment to deal cooperatively with common concerns.

Cross-cultural Communication—refers to the communication process between people of different cultural backgrounds. Culture is viewed as having a major role in the communication process.

Cross-cultural Awareness—a consciousness of the behavior and the ways of thinking and perceiving within another culture. Bringing to the surface unconscious, culturally based assumptions and values held by that culture.

Ecclesiastical Terms

Church—any body of believers who meet together as a congregation for a designated time of worship. They are also recognized by their denomination and/or local body as being a separate and a fully organized cell in the Body of Christ. Gal. 3:26-28 and John 17:21-22 would indicate that a church should strive toward unity of believers despite differences in philosophy, language, values, etc.

Congregation—any body of believers who meet in shared facilities but maintain all the accepted elements of a local church except the recognition by their denomination or governing body as being separate and distinct from other such units within the same facilities.

17

Multicongregation—any church organization where there is the existence of more than one congregation, whether recognized as separately organized or not. This distinction as a congregation is usually for language reasons but can be for racial or ethnic reasons.

Anglo—Webster says that an "Anglo" would be "a Caucasian inhabitant of the United States of non-Latin extraction." With this in mind it is wrong to refer to most English-speaking congregations as "Anglo," since they are sprinkled with people from various ethnic backgrounds. It should be noted that *Anglo-Americans* are an ethnic group and must fit into the definition.

These definitions are not intended to be exhaustive. In most cases the dictionary is very precise and should be consulted.

PART I

CULTURE
and the
CHURCH

Looking at Both Sides
of the Coin

Cultural Diversity and Spiritual Unity

With the large influx of immigrants and refugees into the United States and Canada, many congregations are asking this question: "What is the most responsible way for us to fulfill our ministry to the diverse ethnic and language groups in our community?"

In order to answer that question, it is important that some fundamental truths about the Church be noted and clarified.

English writer John R. W. Stott observes: "The Church is a people, a community of people, who owe their existence, their solidarity, and their corporate distinctness from other communities to one thing only—the call of God."[1]

In Gen. 22:17-18 Abraham was given a "covenant of grace," by which he had originally been called out of his homeland. He was promised that through his people all earth's nations would be blessed. This was fulfilled through Christ.

Through the death and resurrection of Christ, God's purpose is to call out of the world a people for himself and for them to exist with a certain identifiable distinctiveness from the world. God calls us to live a holy life and "to lead a life worthy of the calling to which [we] have been called" (1 Pet. 1:15-16; Eph. 4:1).

But this call to holy living is not a call for the Church to withdraw from the world. Indeed the New Testament declares that the God who called us out of the world has sent us back into the world: "But you are a chosen race, a royal priesthood, a holy nation, God's own people, that you may declare the wonderful deeds of him who called you out of darkness into his marvelous light" (1 Pet. 2:9).

This call is to all His people! It is to the whole Church,

every member, without distinction or partiality. Originally, God's call to Abraham was for His chosen people. Yet even then there was the promise for a blessing to all nations. Paul declares to the Ephesians: "But now in Christ Jesus you who once were far off have been brought near in the blood of Christ. For he is our peace, who has made us both one, and has broken down the dividing wall of hostility, by abolishing in his flesh the law of commandments and ordinances, that he might create in himself one new man in place of the two, so making peace, and might reconcile us both to God in one body through the cross, thereby bringing the hostility to an end" (2:13-16).

Ray Bakke, recognized authority on multicultural ministries in urban settings, points out that: "The Good News is not only that Jesus shed his blood for the world, but also that he got his blood from the world. That is good news especially in a racist society, in a world of yellow, black and brown people."[2]

The Bible more often that not emphasizes cultural and ethnic identity. For example, the opening paragraph of the New Testament makes clear the background of Jesus. The Gospels were very carefully written to identify with a specific cultural group. Matthew wrote his Gospel for the Jews, to present Jesus as the Messiah, while Luke sought to communicate with the Gentiles.

So, in cross-cultural evangelism we have a two-sided coin. Both sides are necessary and legitimate. To ignore our cultural heritage and the heritage of those with whom we work is foolish. But to deny God's call to the ultimate goal of unity within the Church is to ignore the many scriptures pointing in that direction.

1. John R. W. Stott, *One People* (Old Tappan, N.J.: Fleming H. Revell, 1982), 21.

2. Wesley D. Balda, *Heirs of the Same Promise* (Arcadia, Calif.: National Convocation on Evangelizing Ethnic America, 1984), 47.

CULTURE:
Noticing the Difference

A. Cultural Baggage

Have you had the experience of traveling to another country? Perhaps you have welcomed someone else as he has arrived in America for the first time. Although dressed properly and being the picture of a model citizen, each passenger must pass through that one area that is known as "customs inspection." The inspector asks questions about what you are bringing into the country. You answer them as carefully and honestly as possible. Then usually, as if to prove you wrong, he begins to rummage through the opened suitcases. First the clothes, even the guitar case, and finally ripping open the dog-eared cardboard boxes. Everything visible to the scrutinizing eye of the inspector is examined. But there is some baggage he misses every time. It is a person's "cultural baggage." A person's beliefs, attitudes, and rules for proper behavior in his native land are slipped through as if they were invisible luggage. In the new cultural setting it may take a few days for the old baggage to appear. It usually happens when it is least expected.

There are almost as many explanations of what is included in culture as there are anthropologists. But to help our discussion, here are a few that seem to appear in everyone's list:

1. *Customary Behaviors.* One culture expects children to be quiet and allow adults to be in charge, whereas another culture wants children to express themselves and be more in-

dependent. One culture bases much of its belief on the past, depending on the existence of ancestral spirits. Another focuses on living for the present. Still a third might look to the future and set many goals for activities yet to come. All of these are customary behaviors. They determine the way one behaves toward parents, children, and extended family or how one acts out feelings about the past, present, and future.

2. *Assumptions and Values.* Behind the above-mentioned behavior are a set of values and assumptions that have been taught to a cultural group for centuries. These are often changing but are mostly constant within one generation. Our lives are governed by these principles. When we come in contact with people of another culture, our reaction is automatic and unconscious. Contradiction on their part to any of our cultural values will cause us to build walls through which it is impossible to "hear" what is being communicated.

3. *Patterns of Thinking.* On the deeper level of thought patterns there are also differences from one culture to another. These involve such questions as: Do people think deductively or inductively? Are they more intuitive or reason-bound? Do they or do they not admit to emotion in their thought processes? Do they shut out their environment when they think, or do they use it in their thought process? These types of conflicts will especially surface during decision-making meetings.

4. *Communicative Style.* A gesture, a smile, or a touch on the arm may add emphasis to a message or communicate special meaning, but that meaning is not the same in all cultural groups. Some require a wide range of tone and volume in speech, others do not. The distance at which two people carry on a conversation will vary. When you are accustomed to one style, encountering a different style can be confusing, disorienting, and annoying. Even though a person may know how to speak a second language, it is possible to use nonverbal

communication that makes it difficult for people who understand the language to feel comfortable.

Differences in culture cause static but should not be reason for judgment of right or wrong.

If you are planning to enter the adventure of cross-cultural communication, the following three suggestions are for you:

1. Feel secure in and fully identified in your own culture.

2. Be aware of the degree of difference in culture with which you are comfortable.

3. Respect and appreciate cultural differences encountered in others.

B. Cultural Conclusions

In understanding culture and its relationship to the church situation, it will help to remember:

1. Human beings are creators of culture.

2. Each group developed its own culture thousands of years ago, usually in isolation from one another.

3. Each group found its own way to solve mankind's 10 basic problems: food, clothing, shelter, family organization, social organization, government, war and protection, arts and crafts, knowledge and science, and religion.

4. Different groups have solved these basic needs in different ways.

5. There are no absolutely right responses to the majority of these, only right and wrong responses within the culture itself. Cultures are different from one another but not better or worse.

6. Each cultural group has a tendency to think that their culture is superior to other cultures.

7. Parents are correctly doing their cultural duty when they teach children the right ways to do things in their own culture.

8. People generally do not have difficulties within their own culture as long as they obey the rules of that culture. Problems arise when they wander to another culture and try to live without observing the rules of the new culture.

9. Cultural problems and culture shock occur when a person who is inculturated in one cultural view is placed in another culture for a certain length of time and tries to communicate cross-culturally.

C. Culture Shock

Culture shock might be called a disease that occurs among people who are suddenly placed into a situation where they must communicate with other cultures. Like most ailments, it has its own symptoms and cure.

Respected values that have been taught may not be shared with those we meet. We may not know when to shake hands or how to greet one another. Certain gestures might be offensive to us. We can find ourselves in embarrassing situations. Facing confusion and frustration, we find ourselves slipping into culture shock. The key symptoms are:

—a feeling of being lost in a strange environment
—frustration and anxiety
—a desire to reject the other person and/or culture
—a hostile and aggressive attitude regarding the strange culture
—avoiding people of the new culture and associating only with those like ourselves

If patience wins, one starts to adjust in learning about the new culture, getting interested in the people, and putting things into perspective. Finally, the new values, beliefs, and assumptions are learned and accepted as another way.

Culture shock is no longer an experience reserved for overseas missionaries. It is happening in North America and in all other Western nations. Whenever cultures cross, there will be shock. The degree of that shock will depend on the amount of difference between the cultures and the ability of the individuals involved to absorb the change necessary to adjust.

Several tendencies in our culture must be eliminated if we are to adjust to cultural differences in a mature manner.

1. *Ethnocentricism.* Ethnocentricism is a basic response by humans for survival. It is natural for us to cling to our culture. From birth our culture is linked with that which gives us sustenance: our parents, our families, our culture groups. Since strength lies in the group, we believe that our group is right and must be defended. Ethnocentricism is the relatively *blatant* assertion of personal and cultural superiority. Its motto is "My way is the right way!"

For most American churches, cross-cultural contact is new. Until recently, most immigration to America has been from European countries, and adjustment has been relatively simple.

Only a few select people went overseas for missionary service, and they were trained to adjust to the new environment. At first, they were in the same position that most Americans find themselves. They did not know the local language. They did not know the social rules of the land. They made serious cultural errors, inadvertently insulting the people who lived there. Most certainly, souls were lost and contacts for the church were lost because of their ignorance. But many people believed the message of these missionaries, and they continued until they could communicate and function in the new culture.

Americans who stayed in their homeland had no such adjustments to make and did not foresee any need to learn about other cultures firsthand. Then the immigration of the 1970s and 1980s began. Millions of legal and illegal immigrants and refugees poured across our borders. These people came largely from non-European countries. Cross-cultural awareness was necessary for more and more Americans.

To meet the ever-growing challenge of evangelizing the United States and Canada, we must move from self-centered ethnocentricism to a broader acceptance of other cultures.

2. *English Only.* It is often falsely assumed that if we could just teach English to all incoming people, all the cultural differences would be solved. This is not true. Another myth often believed is that if a person has learned our language and has lived here for some time, he understands the sacred values of our language and culture. This is usually not true. Actually, people who relocate here can be grouped in several categories.

First, there are the strict cultural traditionalists. These people are usually old-timers, a dying breed though often still the ones who make the key decisions at home. Some speak only a smattering of English, and many will not learn it at all. Today, a growing number of ethnics are young and nationalistic. They too wish to retain and maintain their language and culture.

Second are those who have chosen to become Americanized or Westernized. They are a younger-generation people who speak English and have been educated in the West. You may be surprised to know that of the three groups, this is the smallest.

The third group is the largest and fastest-growing of all groups. They place somewhere between groups one and two. They speak fluent English, hold degrees from North American universities, and accept Western ways as long as it enables them to get ahead in the system. They are accepting a cultural compromise in order to economically progress.

Somehow we must accept these people without forcing them to adapt to our language and ways. While English is important to us and all who live in North America, we know God understands all languages. He listens most to the language of the soul. We dare not lose one soul to God's kingdom because of limitations we have put upon a group of individuals.

3. *Directness.* North Americans are encouraged to be direct, frank, and concise in getting to the bottom line. If called on to communicate with other cultures, you will no doubt have to adapt your style to conform with the etiquette and customs of that particular people. In *Never Take Yes for an Answer,* Masaaki Imai cites one of the problems in communicating. "A newcomer to Japan may never be able to recover from the initial culture shock of finding out that 'yes' does not always mean 'yes' in Japan until he realizes that there are some sixteen ways to avoid saying 'no' and that to call a spade a spade is not in the Japanese tradition."[1] You can count on similar differences creeping into the value system of Japanese who have settled in Western countries.

4. *Efficiency.* North Americans are shocked to find out there is not as much emphasis put on clock-watching in other cultures. Each culture has their own standard of efficiency, and it in no way reflects on their intelligence, ability, or even desire to make money. Usually it is a matter of different life priorities. It is correctly assumed by them that if you are serious about communicating with them, you will understand, accept, and respect what those priorities are.

5. *People First.* The American culture is one of the few in the world where profits and business come before the interest of people. Most other cultures want to become acquainted and know with whom they are talking before they get down to business. A century ago, when life moved at a slower pace, Americans were the same. Now, even in the church we have a tendency to replace our compassion for people and our desire to get acquainted with efficiency for business principles. We need to be on our guard against this.

6. *Legal System.* Simple trust and personal relationships are key in many cultures. Often a person's word is honored

and will hold a bargain. On the other hand, our high-pressure legal system of juries, judges, and lawyers may be completely strange and alien to another culture. Even Western business meetings (are they really necessary?) may not be understood.

7. *Money.* The necessity for a church to quickly stand on its own and be separate from the mothering body is a good principle, but it is a cultural issue. The superdrive toward independence is part of our background but is not necessarily biblical. It is a concept encouraged in American homes and social life. The concept of tithing is one that is taught by many churches in North America but not always in the overseas congregations. Leaders must have patience in training newcomers in this important principle and must be willing to wait a little longer for some cultures to comprehend it.

D. Bridging: Learning to Cross Cultural Barriers

Cross-cultural relationships are often complicated by our lack of knowledge. We have the desire, but we do not know how to cross the barriers society has erected. To further complicate the matter, many cultures are very ethnocentric and/or prejudiced. To be honest, no one thing nor any one person can solve the intercultural communication problems we all encounter. But the good news is that there are some specific guidelines in approaching them. The conscientious cultural bridge communicator will find them helpful.

1. *Listen.* In working with individuals in the secular or religious world, we learn early that listening is a vital skill. If a person hasn't developed that ability, it is usually because he is more interested in what he has to say than what is being said by another person. He has a tendency to jump to conclusions before statements are completed and is more interested in the meaning of words than in thoughts. People who have not learned to listen and who attempt to work with another culture allow preconceived concepts of the culture to affect their

assumptions about what they are going to say. Positive practice is the only way to overcome this bad habit that leads to wrong interpretation of what is actually being said. *All assumptions* about how a person thinks and how he will behave must be discarded. Speaking to someone in his second language can cause particular difficulty. Be sure to pick up differences not only in inflection but also in meaning. In intercultural communication skillful listening to the verbal and nonverbal messages without filtering them through our own system of values and expectations is an imperative.

2. *Check our perception of the other person.* Our wish to control the conversation or to achieve our objectives may greatly hinder us from pursuing this worthy goal of understanding another. If effective communicating is to take place, we cannot allow what is being said to be clouded by our perception of the other person.

3. *Get feedback.* The possibility of misunderstanding is always present when two different cultures communicate. That is why feedback is so important. In short: Ask if you have been understood! You may be receiving all the facial and even verbal (or hand) gestures that make it appear that the message is understood. But do not assume that communication has taken place. A repeating of the message may be very revealing. Most people who have worked with other cultures for years know that untangling miscommunicated messages is far more difficult than requesting immediate feedback while the communication is taking place.

4. *Cultivate an awareness of your own culture.* It is possible to be too aware of cultural differences and therefore be unable to develop relationships with other cultures. However, the other extreme is harmful also. Be aware of your own behavior patterns, communicative style, assumptions and values, and patterns of thinking. In recognizing your own dis-

tinctiveness, you are more prepared to communicate with others.

5. *Take risks.* Cross-cultural learning takes place best when participants have established enough trust to take risks and to allow for the exposure of themselves. Sometimes intercultural communication requires us to open ourselves to criticism. In our pursuit to communicate, we will be vulnerable to hurtful responses. There is no denying there will be times of miscommunications and feelings of failure. But by trying, we will learn from our efforts and mistakes.

6. *Understanding comes in stages.* Robert G. Hanvey, in an article in the book *Toward Internationalism,* [2] gives four stages of understanding that are usually experienced by those crossing cultures.

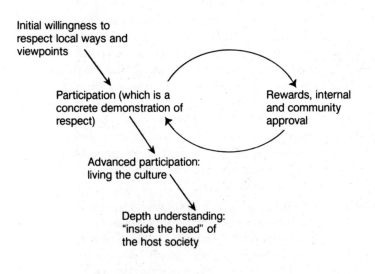

Initial willingness to respect local ways and viewpoints

Participation (which is a concrete demonstration of respect)

Rewards, internal and community approval

Advanced participation: living the culture

Depth understanding: "inside the head" of the host society

To state this in another way, it might be:

LEVEL	INFORMATION	MODE	INTERPRETATION
I	Awareness of superficial or very visible cultural traits stereotypes	Tourism, textbooks, *National Geographic*	Unbelievable, i.e., exotic, bizarre
II	Awareness of significant and subtle cultural traits that contrast markedly with one's own	Culture conflict situations	Unbelievable, i.e., frustrating, irrational
III	Awareness of significant and subtle cultural traits that contrast markedly with one's own	Intellectual analysis	Believable, cognitively
IV	Awareness of how another culture feels from standpoint of the insider	Cultural immersion: living the culture	Believable because of subjective familiarity standpoint of the insider

E. Winning Different Cultures to the Church

Should we weigh down the simple gospel with sociological matters? You have already guessed my feelings from previous pages. There seems to be ample scriptural evidence to show that this type of thought pattern was used in biblical times.

The gospel was originally introduced to the Jews. Paul took the Word to the Jews wherever he traveled. When entering a new city, he went straight to the synagogue. New Testament writing tells us he often avoided cities that did not have Jewish houses of worship.

Have you ever considered what it meant when the gospel was taken to the Samaritans? They came to Christ as Samaritans, without joining Jewish congregations! That was quite a breakthrough in the Jewish customs. God used Peter to penetrate the Gentile world. But it was Paul who was effective in incorporating them into their own culturally oriented churches. So successful was this effort that Acts 15 records the conclusion that Gentiles should not have to be deculturated. These decisions were made from theological viewpoints but have astounding sociological implications. Theologically it said that Gentiles had equal access to God and His kingdom. Sociologically it pointed to a Church that could surround the customs and culture of whatever people group it was reaching. It meant that Gentiles could be discipled within their own language and cultural context.

Ethnic diversity in North American life has been with us in the past, it is with us in the present, and it probably will be around for a long time to come. Both social ethicists and idealistic theologians have tried to convince us that the pluralism in our society is actually unethical. They have claimed that it must be rejected and overcome. Their ultimate dream is built around the melting of all people into one superethnic people. Admittedly, a lot of melting has taken place to form what is now known as the United States and Canada. But most people have a variety of definitions of what makes up citizens of these countries. As long as immigration is allowed to take place, that definition will continue to change. The new flood of legal and illegal immigrants are coming with a new determination to hold on to many of their customs brought from their homeland.

It is my firm belief that God is calling the church to reach people of every ethnic distinction where they are with careful consideration being given to language, culture, and values. It is vital that each denomination, district, and local congregation have an up-to-date plan to evangelize each segment of their area, using knowledge they have regarding each particular culture.

---

1. Masaaki Imai, *Never Take Yes for an Answer* (Tokyo: Simul Press, 1975), 204.

2. Elise C. Smith and Louise Fiber Luce, eds., *Toward Internationalism: Readings in Cross-cultural Communication* (Rowley, Mass.: Newbury House Publishers, 1969), 50-53.

UNITY:

The Basic Ingredient in a Good Stew

It is a true statement: "Every person is in certain respects (a) like all others, (b) like some others, (c) like no other." Kluckhohn and Murray expanded on this idea to define the three dimensions of being human.

1. We are universal beings—"like all others."

2. We are cultural beings—"like some others." Every human being is shaped by the community (country or culture in which he lives). This combination of values, beliefs, customs, religion, and basic life assumptions that is called culture is shared by those who coexist in that community.

3. We are individual beings—"like no other." Every human being is a unique creation of God. He has his own perceptions, feelings, and experiences. There was not, is not, and never will be another that sees, thinks, feels, celebrates, or suffers in the identical way. Each of us is a "one of a kind" human being.[1]

We have touched on No. 2 and No. 3 in the first section. There are many more things that could be said. But it is important to understand that there are more things that make humans alike than things that make them different. Nothing that happens within one human being is completely foreign to another.

The great number of common experiences in each culture are evidenced in the work of Yale University's Human Relations Area Files, which have since 1936 collected material from over 300 cultures. These files now list the following categories of items that are universal in all the cultures they have studied:[2]

Age grading
Athletic sports
Bodily adornment
Calendar
Cleanliness training
Community organization
Cooking
Cooperative labor
Cosmology
Courtship
Dancing
Decorative art
Divination
Division of labor
Dream interpretation
Education
Eschatology
Ethics
Ethnobotany
Etiquette
Faith healing
Family
Feasting
Fire making
Food taboos
Funeral rites
Games
Gestures
Gift giving
Government
Greetings

Hairstyles
Hospitality
Housing
Hygiene
Incest taboos
Inheritance rules
Joking
Kin groups
Kinship
Language
Law
Luck superstitions
Magic
Marriage
Medicine
Modesty concerning
    natural functions
Mournings
Music
Mythology
Numerals
Obstetrics
Penal sanctions
Personal names
Population policy
Postnatal care
Pregnancy usages
Property rights
Propitiation of super-
    natural beings
Puberty customs

Religious ritual
Residence rules
Sexual restrictions
Soul concerns
Status differences
Surgery

Toolmaking
Trade
Visiting
Weaning
Weather control

A. We Are One Human Race

There are four basic areas in which all human beings share common traits:

1. *We are biologically similar.* Even if one wants to divide people according to race, a correct understanding is necessary. There are basically only three races: Caucasoid, Negroid, and Mongoloid. To classify and divide ethnic groups into "different races" is incorrect.

Various scholars argue that the very attempt to divide humans by color (the basis of racial division) is not worthy of discussion. They point out that the stereotyped differences of color, features, and stature are inconsequential when one notes that human anatomy (including blood types), reproduction, and all bodily functions are primarily the same worldwide. Even though each ethnic group share different biological problems and care for them in different ways, we are basically the same.

2. *Intellectual capacity is common.* Perception, memory, reasoning, emotion, and volition are almost identical among all humans. This is true also of rationalization, projection, attribution, denial, and reaction formation.

3. *We are all spiritual beings.* Not only is the gospel universal but also is the need for all humans to receive and be transformed by that gospel. All cultures have some religion. This is, at base, a reaching out for the true and living God. A sense of the transcendent, of moral values, of some kind of a

symbolic eternity, of explanations for the presence of good and evil are found in all human beings.

4. *Cultures as created by humans are intriguingly parallel in patterns.* Of course, the biological, intellectual, and spiritual similarities already noted make up much of the culture of mankind. Most differences in cultures are in forms of logic, rather than in basic needs.

B. The Bible Teaches That We Are One

Because God is one, all who are God's are one. J. S. Whale writes: "He [man] is lifted above all other earthly creatures in being made in the image of God, and in being aware of the fact. He is aware that the Creator is the Eternal Love who calls men into existence that their willing response to his love may fulfill his creative purpose."[3] Man was not created as different races and/or cultures. He was created as a human being for fellowship with God. The biblical statement is that "God created man" (Gen. 1:27), and it points to the unity of man and woman (2:7). Augustine wrote (concerning the unity of mankind) that God propagated the whole human race from one individual, namely Adam, while all other species were started by multiple creation. "Man ... He created one and alone, not indeed that he should live in isolation, outside human society, but in the unity of that society."[4]

The Bible shows our unity first by our relationship to God. We are godlike beings, created by His will in His image. The qualities that tie us to the created will of God are the qualities that separate us from the rest of the animal kingdom, namely, rational, moral, and spiritual qualities.

The second unique quality that points to our unity flows directly from the first. We are to live in unity with all men. The God who made humankind is himself a social being, one God in eternal relationship with himself in the three distinct Persons of the Trinity. He said, "Let us make man in our image" (Gen. 1:26). The creation of God is designed to bring man together. Sexuality brings man and woman together. Friendship brings people of various sexes together. The Church is God's creation to bring all people together as a demonstration of the Godhead.

The third distinctive quality of our unity is found in our relationship to the earth and its creatures. God gave us dominion over the earth. But even in our stewardship God calls on mankind to show a unity to properly administer the earth that He has given us.

C. God's Church Is One Church

God has instructed the Church to go and spread the gospel to all nations. This instruction is to the whole Church. Before Christ's coming to earth the calling had been to Abraham and his descendants, to physical, national Israel. Gentiles had been "alienated from the commonwealth of Israel, and strangers to the covenants of promise" (Eph. 2:12). Now this message was to include all nations. That is why Paul went on to write verses 13-16 (quoted at the beginning of Part I) concerning "one new man." This "one new man" created by God is the Church. Christ has abolished the racial and nationalistic barriers. He has removed the class and sex barriers also: "There is neither Jew nor Greek, there is neither slave nor free, there is neither male nor female; for you are all one in Christ Jesus" (Gal. 3:28). Paul announces that the days of discrimination are over. The Church will tolerate no distinction of race, rank, or sex. All spiritual privilege given by God is open to everyone. "For there is no distinction . . . the same Lord is Lord of all and bestows his riches upon all who call upon him. For, 'every one who calls upon the name of the Lord will be saved'" (Rom. 10:12-13).

Because of this all Christian believers are "fellow citizens with the saints and members of the household of God" (Eph.

2:19), and again "fellow heirs, members of the same body, and partakers of the promise in Christ Jesus through the gospel" (3:6). Paul combines Greek compound words (fellow citizens, fellow heirs, fellow members, and fellow partakers) to illustrate the common participation of all of God's people in the blessings of the gospel. The same truth is taught in 4:4-6: "There is one body and one Spirit, just as you were called to the one hope that belongs to your call, one Lord, one faith, one baptism, and God and Father of us all, who is above all and through all and in all."

When Jesus illustrates the Kingdom with various parables (Mark 2:18-20, expanded in Eph. 5:22-33; Mark 12; John 15; and Luke 15:3-7), He points to the relationship that God has established with His people:

1. God's people are His dominion. He has established a way to unify all His people: through the Church.

2. God's people are His family. We are adopted into God's family and given His Spirit that we may call Him "Abba, Father" (Rom. 8:15; Gal. 4:6, both KJV). We are to unite ourselves within this family and feel the relationship with all other family members.

3. God's people are His building, "a holy temple in the Lord" (Eph. 2:21), a construction of God himself.

4. God's people are the Body of Christ. This is the most prominent image given by Paul in his writings and the only one without Old Testament equivalent. Christ, the Head, unites all those that are different into one Body functioning for one purpose.

D. The Bond That Makes Us One: Holy Living

The Scriptures are full of verses pointing to a Church that is distinct from other peoples. God is interested in a church united and is repeatedly telling that Church: "I will be your God, and you shall be My people" (see 2 Cor. 6:16). The char-

41

acter of each member of the Church is not what makes him different from other Church members but what distinguishes him from the rest of mankind (spiritually speaking). And because God's people are "peculiar" ("different"; 1 Pet. 2:9, KJV), they are called to show their difference in their behavior. "I am the Lord your God. You shall not do as they do in the land of Egypt, where you dwelt, and you shall not do as they do in the land of Canaan, to which I am bringing you. You shall not walk in their statutes. You shall do my ordinances and keep my statutes and walk in them. I am the Lord your God" (Lev. 18:2-4). Jesus called His disciples to holy living in much the same manner: "You know that the rulers of the Gentiles lord it over them, and their great men exercise authority over them. It shall not be so among you" (Matt. 20:25-26). Paul follows the same call to be holy in Eph. 4:17: "You must no longer live as the Gentiles do." To Jesus, unity and equality were features of the "called-out ones." They were to begin to train themselves to think this way in order to fit into the culture of the kingdom of God.

The Church must not get caught in the trap of looking within itself for differences. The differentiation is not in the Church but from the world. We are one with each other but separate from the world because we are holy unto the Lord.

Conclusion

In the midst of all the unity that is expected from the Church, differences do still exist. Some of these differences are cultural; some are functional. Paul talks about a single human body consisting of many parts. For example: "For as in one body we have many members, and all the members do not have the same function, so we, though many, are one body in Christ, and individually members one of another. Having gifts that differ according to the grace given to us, let us use them" (Rom. 12:4-6). Paul elaborates further on this in 1 Corinthians 12 where he begins by celebrating our unity in the Spirit. He then shows that we have different graces and gifts for service. All these gifts are bestowed by the one Spirit that unites us in one body.

The same unity is possible for cultural differences. Mark Edward Oh in his doctoral dissertation says:

> The solution was not conceived in the wicked heart of man, but was given from above again—Yhwh, the Incarnate logos in Christ! That is the CROSS culture! What had been "separated and dispersed" on the earth at the Tower of Babel culture has been reunited in the CROSS culture, which I would call, "Christ culture," with Christ's attitudes, His values, and His ways of behaving (Phil. 2:5-11), serving the Lord and one another in humility, speaking the language of love and care, and walking in the Lord Jesus Christ by the Holy Spirit to the praise of His glory.[5]

It is possible that the Tower of Babel symbolizes God's plan for decentralization of people who tried to centralize humanity. But the cross of Jesus Christ symbolizes God's design for unity in diversity through His revelation and reconciliation of humanity in Christ.

In the next part we will study the multicongregational model that allows God to work among our diversity to lead us into unity by His Spirit.

---

1. Clyde Kluckhohn and Henry Murray, *Personality in Nature, Society, and Culture* (New York: Alfred A. Knopf, 1948).

2. George Peter Murdock, *Outline of Cultural Materials* (New Haven, Conn.: Human Relation Area Files, 1961).

3. John S. Whale, *Christian Doctrine* (New York: Macmillan Co., 1941), 44.

4. Werner Stark, *Social Theory and Christian Thought* (London: Routledge and Kegan Paul, 1959), 7.

5. Mark E. Oh, "Cultural Pluralism and Multiethnic Congregation as a Ministry Model in an Urban Society" (D.Min. diss., Fuller Theological Seminary, 1988).

PART II

THE MULTI-CONGREGATIONAL CHURCH

A Model

In Part I of this book we have seen that man is a creation of God as well as a product of the culture in which he is existing. Because of this he is best evangelized within the comfort of his language and surroundings. But we as a Church must not be satisfied with less than unity in the Body of Christ.

The United States and Canada have seen unbelievable change in the last 170 years. Europe, for the first 140 years, was the main source of immigrants to our shores. In the last 30 years people have immigrated here from nearly every country of the world!

I do not need to convince you of the cultural and lingual diversity in Canada and the United States or the need for churches among the various groups represented here.

So now let us consider the multicongregational model and imagine what it could do for church planting in these countries.

A. The Challenge of the Multicongregation

In one study conducted by the research division of the Church of the Nazarene, the effect of the multicongregational approach to church planting was considered.

In 1895 the Church of the Nazarene was founded as a multicongregational church by Dr. P. F. Bresee. Spanish- and Chinese-language congregations were housed in the original church in Los Angeles.

By 1976 few other churches had used this model. However, in the next 10 years this had grown until nearly 150 churches were making multiple use of their facilities to reach out to the diverse ethnic populations surrounding them.

In a recent meeting of Nazarene denominational leaders the question was asked: "What is the potential of the multicongregational model in planting churches among various cultural and language groups in Canada and the United States?" Complete demographic information was not available that would answer this question. Therefore, the following facts were gathered:

1. Counties with 2,500 or more of one particular ethnic minority group were located.

2. Next, counties were eliminated that already have at least one Nazarene congregation among that particular ethnic group.

3. Counties were also eliminated if they did not have any Churches of the Nazarene with facilities that could house a multicongregation.

The report revealed these facts:

ETHNIC GROUP STUDIED	QUALIFYING COUNTIES	POTENTIAL MULTICONGREGATIONS
Hispanic	249	758
Japanese	29	233
Asian/E. Indian/ Indo Pak.	29	179
Filipino	41	263
Korean	12	31
Total Minimal Potential		1,664

This did not locate all potential areas for multicongregational church planting. It left out some of the key population areas for church planting among ethnics because ethnic churches were already established there (such as Los Angeles, Chicago, New York, etc.).

The only reliable statistics available for this study were from the 1980 census figures. In most areas of heavy concentrations of ethnics these figures are changing and growing rapidly. A similar study of the 1990 U.S. Census figures will doubtless reveal an even greater potential for the multicongregational model to be used in church planting and growth.

The figure of 1,664 potential church starts is unbelievable when we realize that this denomination has started only 655 churches in the 12 years between 1976 and 1987 (622 in the U.S. and 33 in Canada)!

The most exciting part is that these churches could be planted with very little cost in facility renovation. And the bonus is that it will fulfill Christ's command to promote unity within the Church.

B. Is This Model Biblical?

We have already taken time to look at the desire of God to have His people one. There are many biblical examples of how He accomplished this while allowing the diversity of individual cultural differences.

1. *The Trinity.* The Bible is very clear on the personality of each Person of the Trinity. The Father guided much of the activity of the Old Testament period. Then He lovingly cared for Jesus during His time on earth. Jesus, the Logos, was with God and was God "in the beginning" (John 1:1). The Holy Spirit, the Communicator of the message from God, lives in and through each person who allows Him to do so. Yet as D. Stuart Briscoe points out, the significance of the Trinity is in "a wholeness" and a "completeness about God in His three person-relatedness which made Him totally self-sufficient."[1]

2. *The 12 Tribes of Israel.* Coming from one person, these 12 brothers were all given the same covenant. However,

as the children of Israel grew in numbers, the functions of the various tribes became apparent. *A Dictionary of the Bible and Christian Doctrine in Everyday English* gives a clear explanation of the significance of this illustration: "The tribes of Israel were groups of families. The tribes formed one nation. They shared a common history and religion. . . . The Book of Revelation uses the phrase 'tribes of Israel.' It means all the people of God of all time (Revelation 7:4-8). The New Testament also uses 'twelve tribes' to represent the whole Christian Church."[2] From the Scriptures we learn that the main time of gathering together for these 12 culturally different tribes was at public worship. They must have functioned somewhat like a multi-congregation, feeling unity in God's presence.

3. *The 12 Disciples.* Jesus' ministry seemed to be limited to His own people, the Jews. But within that culture He chose 12 men from different backgrounds. One can imagine the difficulty of unifying fishermen and tax collectors. Jesus prayed to the Father in John 17 that the disciples would "be one, even as we are one" (John 17:11). He then sent them out into the world to evangelize all nations with the same goal of being one in spirit. Jesus Christ was illustrating the type of unity that can take place within His Church.

4. *The Birth of the Church (Acts 2).* Peter on the Day of Pentecost preached to the congregation from many nations, divided by culture and language. Even though the Christian Church was born in the midst of cultural pluralism (the first 3,000 converts being from all parts of the civilized world), an amazing unity existed in the midst of diversity. This was accomplished by the power of the Holy Spirit. Yet there was careful planning on the part of the disciples to make sure they brought people into contact with one another. It was not all automatic just because of the indwelling of the Holy Spirit.

5. *The Church at Antioch.* In Acts 11:19 a new group of believers, mostly scattered Jewish people, had begun to meet.

Before long this group began to reach out to the many cultural groups living in the city of Antioch. A few more verses recount the number in the church growing to represent most of the segments of the city. But this medley of cultures met together to worship one God. It is no surprise that by chapter 13 they had become an established congregation and were the sending group to spread the gospel to new cities across that area.

6. *The Book of Revelation.* The apostle John describes heaven as seen in his vision as "a great multitude which no man could number, from every nation, from all tribes and peoples and tongues, standing before the throne and before the Lamb" (Rev. 7:9). John saw the tribes and nations retaining their ethnic identity even in heaven. Once again, they gathered for worship of the Lamb of God, Jesus.

The Bible is filled with illustrations of oneness in the midst of assorted cultures. God loves each of us just the way we are. He is pleased when we put aside our individual prejudices and really love one another. The ideal place to practice this is in our worship before God.

---

1. D. Stuart Briscoe, *Genesis,* vol. 1 in *The Communicator's Commentary,* Lloyd J. Ogilvie, ed. (Waco, Tex.: Word Books, Publisher, 1983), 34.

2. Albert Truesdale et al., eds., *A Dictionary of the Bible and Christian Doctrine in Everyday English* (Kansas City: Beacon Hill Press of Kansas City, 1986), 311.

I

Understanding the Task

Before beginning a multicongregation, it is essential that you understand your own philosophy of ministry and the congregation that is to be planted. It will be helpful for you to get to know as many facts about your community as possible. The following will help you in determining the reason you need to begin another work.

A. Know Your Mission

As persons we are each an original. Because of this God has a unique purpose for each one of us on Earth. It is exciting to think that out of over 5 billion people, God has individually planned a task for each one of us to perform. What a joy to know that the world can be a little richer because we have spent some time here. It is particularly important to face life with *enthusiasm.* This word is derived from two Greek words, *en theos,* meaning "in God."

Richard Nelson Bolles, in his book *What Color Is Your Parachute?* talks of three stages of learning our mission.

1. "Your first Mission here on Earth . . . is to seek out and find, in daily—even hourly—communication, the One from whom your Mission is derived."[1]

Our first and most important mission in life is to discover God in a real and meaningful way. This may seem rather elementary. However, some of us have attended educational institutions and even joined churches whose disciplines teach us a "church culture." This often makes it difficult for God to lead us in new and creative ministries that could be His design for meeting the needs of today's world. We must forget the idea that our mission on earth is to keep busy. Many people need to pause and be quiet before the Lord and learn to "be" before we "do." We need to seek a greater vision of who God really is. He is far beyond and above anything that we can ask or think. It was this God, in the person of Jesus, who said, "I assure you that the man who believes in me will do the same things that I have done, yes, and he will do even greater things than these" (John 14:12, Phillips).

The devil tries to hinder us from understanding this step in finding our mission. He encourages us to think of our earthly existence in physical terms: what we buy, whom we impress, the people we lead, and what we eat, drink, and possess. But we are useless until we have comprehended our mission through a spiritual communication with God that is beyond the ordinary. We must know a Spirit, a Person from beyond the physical who is with us and in us, and with whom we will spend eternity. If we are not willing to spend the time to accomplish this first step in our mission, we cannot see the miracles necessary to bring about cross-cultural communication and coexistence in the unity of God's Spirit.

Even if you have made this first step, review your relationship with a loving and caring God and renew your commitment to Him.

2. "Your second Mission here on Earth is . . . to do what you can moment by moment, day by day, step by step, to make this world a better place—following the leading and guidance of God's Spirit within you and around you."[2]

Can you imagine for a moment that you are walking downtown in a large city. A car speeds by, and some debris is thrown in your eyes. Panic sweeps over you as you realize you are temporarily blind. Standing on the curb, listening to the clamor, you feel completely disoriented and very alone. Suddenly, out of the city's noise a familiar voice of a friend breaks through the gloom and offers to take you home. What relief you feel as you allow him to lead you—one step at a time—down the street you cannot see. Yet, because he is your friend, you trust him—and know he will take you safely home.

This story is similar to the life of a Christian worker stepping out into cross-cultural ministry. Jesus is our Friend, and He has perfect knowledge of our situation. We can feel secure as we put our trust in Him. He will lead us to our destination.

This is an easy-to-understand illustration of our second step in finding our mission. When we ask the question, "What is our mission?" we often expect to be given a panoramic view of the future. From this we hope to grab the design God has in mind for us—where every path is leading—along with detailed steps for the way ahead. But God does not choose to work that way. He wants us to trust Him to lead us one step at a time. That is faith in action.

But for our own good, God keeps us in the valley. One speaker aptly pointed out that there are only a few people who actually live on the mountaintops. Have you noticed that most of the homes and productive farms are on lower ground? "Your mission is to take one step at a time, even when you don't yet see where it all is leading or what the Grand Plan is, or what your overall Mission in life is. Trust Me; I will lead you."[3] The Hebrews definition of faith seems to fit into this purpose of our walk: "Now faith is the assurance of things hoped for, the conviction of things not seen" (11:1).

Actually, these decisions are key in dealing with the multicultural diversity of Canada and the U.S. Daily decisions in the areas of gratitude, kindness, forgiveness, honesty, and love are necessary. We must decide our direction based on His guidance for that day, not on blanket, culturally influenced rules. God may give you one of those rare mountaintop experiences where you will be able to see over to the other side. More than likely, He will not. God works through the little things to make us more responsible when the bigger decisions come along (Luke 16:10-12; 19:11-27). The virtues just listed must become part of our daily patterns before God will trust us to bring unity and peace to a troubled church.

This step also includes learning and training. There are few cross-cultural missionaries in North America today. Many pastors and Christian workers that find themselves in ethnic pockets are untrained for the delicate situations they may face day by day.

The overall goal of the cross-cultural training for leadership must be to provide a framework where leaders can develop skills and acquire knowledge to function effectively in a multicultural environment. This will not happen naturally. There must be a plan set down to accomplish the following goals:

a. To expand cultural awareness. This includes an understanding of an individual's own culture and how it effects decisions.

b. To increase tolerance and acceptance of different values, attitudes, and behaviors.

c. To try to develop an acceptance of all cultures.

d. To develop communication skills that can be used interculturally.

e. To integrate our learning with contact with other cultures.

f. To allow for the personal adjustments needed in such experiences and the stress involved.

g. To seek out new information whenever possible to further expand knowledge.

The leader that follows this plan will often find God leading into areas of instructing other church members on having better relationships with ethnics in the area they are living.

    3. "Your third Mission here on Earth is . . .

        a. to exercise that Talent which you particularly came to Earth to use—your greatest gift which you most delight to use,

        b. in those place(s) or setting(s) which God has caused to appeal to you the most,

        c. and for those purposes which God most needs to have done in the world."[4]

God does not lead us into areas that we are unable to handle with the talents and gifts He has given to us. We will find ourselves given the task and soon find that God will give us the training and instruction to fulfill it.

It may surprise you, but God sometimes gives us our greatest task in an area in which we cannot financially exist without other means. For example, we may have a talent to communicate with people from other cultures, but it is impossible to support our family through that vocation. God often equips us with another talent that will assist in our financial support while we fulfill His central call.

If we know God personally and realize that we do have a purpose for existing, then we will find it easy to find our mission. Our life will take on a new meaning. I have a firm belief that God is leading new and fresh leaders into ministry for the multicultural and multilingual groups in Canada and the United States.

B. Look at the Fields

It has been more than 20 years since the historic Congress on World Evangelism in Berlin in 1966. This congress led to an even larger International Congress of World Evangelization (ICOWE) held in Lausanne, Switzerland, in 1974. In 1985, stemming from a call from ICOWE, the National Convocation of Evangelizing Ethnic America met in Houston. Representatives from 47 denominations were present. Ten general ethnic committees worked to present material aimed at evangelizing ethnic America. It is difficult to know the impact that this convocation had upon these denominations and their leadership. Those attending gained a new vision for the harvest field in Canada and the U.S. They were challenged to view the Book of Acts as a guidebook for reaching people groups that have migrated to our doorsteps.

One term that seems to permeate the literature from each of these conferences (popularized by Dr. Ralph Winter of William Carey International University in Pasadena, Calif.) is *people groups*. In a book designed for these conferences, *people groups* are defined as: "A significantly large grouping of individuals who perceive themselves to have a common affinity for one another because of their shared language, religion, ethnicity, residence, occupation, class, or situation (or combinations of these)."[5] Although the above list could not always be used to choose congregational groupings within a church, it will be helpful to understand shared experiences in seeking ways to evangelize your neighborhood. Dayton suggests identifying them with the chart on the following page.

The ultimate task for the cross-cultural church planter is not the identifying and separating of people groups. *The final task is the unity of all believers.* To forget this will bring frustration and meaninglessness to your task. The Bible is never wrong in its goals. Obey them. Unite the people under the banner of Christ.

---

1. Richard Nelson Bolles, *What Color Is Your Parachute?* (Berkeley, Calif.: Ten Speed Press, 1988), 295-96.

2. Ibid., 296.

3. Ibid., 303.

4. Ibid., 296.

5. Edward R. Dayton, *That Everyone May Hear* (Monrovia, Calif.: Missions Advanced Research and Communication Center, 1983), 18.

REACHING THE UNREACHED PEOPLE GROUPS IN _____
(country, state, province)

| | SON OF MAN, WHAT DO YOU SEE? | | | "... SON OF MAN, CAN THESE BONES LIVE?" Ezekiel 37:3 | |
Name of People Group	Where Are They Located?	How Many People in This Group?	Their Present Religion	What Do You Know About Them?	How Can They Best Be Reached?

2

How Do I Know I Need the Multicongregational Model?

The multicongregational model should not be tried in every situation. Several questions should be pondered before entering such an arrangement. Answering these questions may be a painful process, but not as painful as if you don't.

QUESTION NO. 1:
DO YOU KNOW YOUR COMMUNITY?

A number of good books can guide leadership through the process of understanding the community. *Missions Have Come Home to America: The Church's Cross-cultural Ministry to Ethnics,* by Jerry L. Appleby, and *The Mission Action Sourcebook,* by Raymond W. Hurn, can give you some helpful outlines for surveying various aspects of the community around your church.

QUESTION NO. 2:
HAS YOUR CHURCH DEVELOPED ITS PHILOSOPHY OF ADMINISTRATIVE CONTROL?

R. A. Schermerhorn did some interesting research out of Case Western Reserve University some years ago. In his book *Comparative Ethnic Relations* he explores the conditions that foster or prevent the integration of ethnic groups with one another. He gives an interesting definition of integration as "a process whereby units or elements of a society are brought into an active and coordinated compliance with the ongoing activities and objectives of the dominant group."[1] Such a definition opens a whole range of possible actions and emotions depending on the attitude of the planting church in relationship to the planted church (see chart on page 61).

Schermerhorn goes on to define what he calls the "superordinate" group as the group that assumes control, whether legitimately or not. The "subordinate" is the group not in control. The immediate question posed on the chart on the next page is: How is this authority or lack of it viewed by the members on both sides? This question is extremely important to the success or failure of a multicongregation. If the planting church is not willing to surrender some of the dominance, they need to understand that there are certain ethnic groups who will not stay around very long.

Another key question is raised by Schermerhorn. Do the interacting groups have centripetal or centrifugal tendencies? Centripetal tendencies "refer both to cultural trends such as acceptance of common values, styles of life, etc., as well as structural features like increased participation in a common set of groups, associations, and institutions." Conversely, centrifugal tendencies "are those that foster separation from the dominant group or from societal bonds in one respect or another. Culturally this most frequently means retention and preservation of the group's distinctive traditions in spheres like language, religion, recreation, etc., together with the particularistic values associated with them."[2] See chart on page 62.

It is easy to see that the greatest amount of satisfaction comes when both (or all) groups agree on an administrative policy regarding authority in the church and live with it. When both groups want to have the same goals and directions of ministry, there is greater satisfaction than when both groups

MULTICONGREGATION EFFECTIVENESS AND ATTITUDES OF AND ABOUT POWER OF DOMINANT GROUP

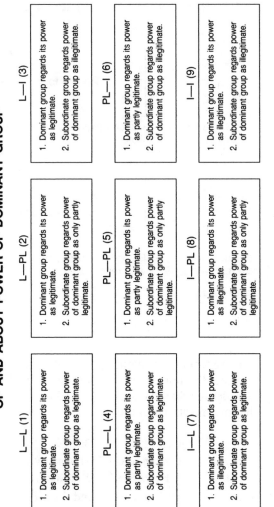

L—L (1)
1. Dominant group regards its power as legitimate.
2. Subordinate group regards power of dominant group as legitimate.

PL—L (4)
1. Dominant group regards its power as partly legitimate.
2. Subordinate group regards power of dominant group as legitimate.

I—L (7)
1. Dominant group regards its power as illegitimate.
2. Subordinate group regards power of dominant group as legitimate.

L—PL (2)
1. Dominant group regards its power as legitimate.
2. Subordinate group regards power of dominant group as only partly legitimate.

PL—PL (5)
1. Dominant group regards its power as partly legitimate.
2. Subordinate group regards power of dominant group as only partly legitimate.

I—PL (8)
1. Dominant group regards its power as illegitimate.
2. Subordinate group regards power of dominant group as only partly legitimate.

L—I (3)
1. Dominant group regards its power as legitimate.
2. Subordinate group regards power of dominant group as illegitimate.

PL—I (6)
1. Dominant group regards its power as partly legitimate.
2. Subordinate group regards power of dominant group as illegitimate.

I—I (9)
1. Dominant group regards its power as illegitimate.
2. Subordinate group regards power of dominant group as illegitimate.

First letter = self-definition of superordinate
Second letter = other-definition of subordinate

L = Definition of superordination as legitimate
PL = Definition of superordination as partially legitimate
I = Definition of superordination as illegitimate

61

CENTRIPETAL AND CENTRIFUGAL TRENDS OF SUBORDINATES IN MULTICONGREGATIONS

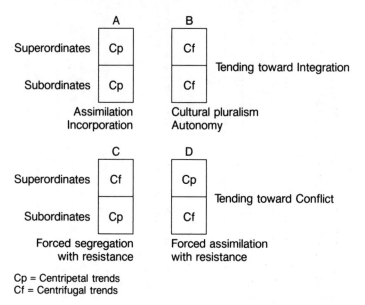

Cp = Centripetal trends
Cf = Centrifugal trends

desire to stay separate and maintain a "renter" philosophy. However, it should be noted here that the "renter" philosophy is more to be desired than the tension caused by a group feeling that they are misplaced in the ladder of authority.

QUESTION NO. 3:
WHAT IS THE PHILOSOPHY OF AUTHORITY OF THE PLANTED CHURCH'S LEADERSHIP?

The charts on page 61 and above and the accompanying explanation seem to cover this subject. The only caution is that both pastors sit down with a third party (preferably from the district leadership) who will restate what is decided to avoid misunderstanding.

Language can create a problem. A particular concern is negotiation between leaders who only partially understand one another. Language translation is important, even if it is done by a nonprofessional interpreter.

These decisions should take place before services start on a shared basis.

QUESTION NO. 4:
CAN YOU AND YOUR PEOPLE DEAL WITH DIFFICULT ETHICAL ISSUES?

How will your church handle the issue of illegal aliens? For example, will you be able to have patience with a new convert who is married for immigration purposes and cannot divorce without being deported? This sounds simple until you realize that this person is living with another partner and has three children by this second partner. All the children were born in the U.S. and possibly could not go with the parents back to the country of origin. Unfortunately, life is tough for people who are illegally in this country. And going home is not that easy.

Many times questions on immigration cannot be easily answered. There are circumstances that seem unfair. There are times we must just love the people and not try to answer questions that are not being asked.

QUESTION NO. 5:
CAN YOU HANDLE THE LONELINESS OF NOT BEING UNDERSTOOD BY YOUR NEIGHBORHOOD CHURCHES?

A recent communication from several urban and multicongregational pastors showed a feeling that very few understood what they were going through.

Many authorities believe it is good to start two or more multicongregational churches in an area at one time. This allows the pastors to compare notes and receive fellowship with understanding.

Ezra Earl Jones and Robert Wilson combined to author a book called *What's Ahead for Old First Church.* They argue that the success or failure of downtown churches depends on three factors: (1) The church must be located where its potential constituency is derived; (2) the church must have sufficient resources and leadership for ministry in the inner city; and (3) the church must decide to act in time to reverse its situation by taking positive steps for future growth. They write that "the [church] that will still be viable . . . will be the one that has the three factors in favorable combination. It will be located in a place accessible to its potential constituency. It will have members whose theological understanding of the church and whose openness to change enable the congregation to embark on new ministries. It will have enough people to provide the necessary leadership and support. And finally, the congregation will have had sufficient time to determine what its ministry in the changing downtown will be and to marshal its forces for the change."[3]

Many of the same suggestions must be made for the multicongregation. The church may or may not be in the city. But it should be ready for change and adjustment.

If a people look at their neighborhood and discover a sizable pocket of one or more ethnic groups, it is most advisable that they begin steps to plant a sister church in their facility according to the guidelines outlined in the following chapter.

1. R. A. Schermerhorn, *Comparative Ethnic Relations* (Chicago: University of Chicago Press, 1979), 66.

2. Ibid., 81.

3. Ezra Earl Jones and Robert Wilson, *What's Ahead for Old First Church* (New York: Harper and Row, 1974), 7-8.

3

Issues Involved in Sharing Facilities

The following list of issues was adapted with permission from an outline by Dr. Fletcher Tink. It is meant not to be all-inclusive but to serve as a guide with leaders as they discuss multiple use of their facility. Several multicongregational pastors have contributed items in the hope that others will learn from their experiences.

A. Facility Use Issues

For many churches, sharing their building is the most difficult item to face with another congregation. Often churches have shifted from people centeredness to building centeredness. In the process of trying to attract more people to our beautiful facilities, we have left some people unable to meaningfully relate to their surroundings.

But the problem is not with our buildings but with our misplaced sentiment for these facilities. One district superintendent joked: "We operate our church like a McDonald's franchise." He went on to explain how we give our money to God and even dedicate our facilities to Him. Then we demand control of it. The people of each church must answer this question: "Whose church is it, anyway?"

Not all big, ornate buildings are bad. No! But it is important to note that in a multicongregation:

1. People must take precedence over buildings.

2. Buildings should be simply designed so that individuals who have a meager standard of living will not be alienated. And,

3. People must really decide that God owns the building, and He must be consulted regarding their use of it.

Some pertinent questions to be answered before entering into a multicongregational arrangement must include:

—What rooms/buildings are to be used by each group?

—When are these rooms/buildings to be used? Are they to be on a first-come basis or when not used by the super-ordinate congregation?

—What equipment (musical instruments, offering plates, flags, hymnbooks, office equipment, vans) is to be shared, moved, or have exclusive use by one group only?

—Who will hold legal title for the buildings and therefore be responsible for insurance, damage and repairs, and payments?

—Who is responsible for the opening and locking up of the buildings?

—Who takes care of custodial services?

—Who pays for the damage or misuse of facilities and equipment?

—Who has final say on flowers, decorations, and special day arrangements?

—Who makes plans and votes on expansion and remodeling of facilities?

—Does the pastor of each congregation get an office?

—Is the secretary available for work from all congregations?

—Are there enough phone lines? Is it necessary to have someone in the office who is bilingual?

—Are there any restrictions regarding certain activities in certain parts of the church facility?

—Will one church sign be in several languages? Will there be several church signs?

—Can a subordinate congregation obligate themselves to loans on property or equipment? What permission is necessary? (Is there adequate understanding of denominational regulations?)

B. Program Issues

Worship styles are another precious cultural item to many churches. It is important to note that different people groups worship in different ways. Hand clapping may replace "Amen." Tambourines, drums, and electric guitars may be used instead of a piano and an organ. "Freedom of the Spirit" may dictate service length rather than the clock. If your people are properly prepared and if the right questions are asked, smooth handling of more than one service can be a reality.

Think it over and discuss items that pertain to the program in your church, including these questions:

—Will the services meet at different times or in different locations?

—If the services are at different times, who will have first preference? Remember, much heartache will be saved if you let the group who tend to have longer services go last. Your people can adjust to an earlier service easier than they can adjust to waiting every Sunday for the use of the sanctuary.

—Are the beginning and ending times of the services realistic? Have we taken into account altar calls, special speakers, children's programs, films, etc.?

—Have we allowed for fellowship times between congregations?

—Are there planned united worship experiences? How often are these experiences? If the worship time is different, whose service yields to the other?

—Will English be the primary language of these combined services with interpretation, or will each congregation have a short time to speak in their language (five minutes or so) with songs sung in all languages represented?

—Will you have rituals together, that is, baptism, infant dedication, prayer, Holy Communion, church membership rites, ritual meals, musical celebrations, etc.? Do all pastors have proper license to perform the church rituals?

—Will there be outreach literature shared by the congregations? Will it be in the language of each group? How will the cost be divided?

—Will Sunday School be separate or together? How will teachers and staff be chosen? Do the children and/or youth receive their public education in English and therefore prefer their Sunday School in English? What are the preferences of the parents?

—Will other Christian education experiences be shared, such as Vacation Bible School, parenting classes, Marriage Encounter seminars, day-care program, English as a Second Language classes, multilanguage church library?

—Will united evangelistic ventures be tried, such as revivals, trips to encourage nearby churches including maybe a combined choir, trips to foreign countries?

—Have greeters and ushers in each congregation been properly trained to direct people to the right place at the right time, including child care?

—Is nursery, children's church, etc., to be shared by the congregations?

—Have cultural tension points been discussed, such as cleanup, kitchen, discipline of children, proper use of rest rooms, parking properly, etc.?

—Are there other tasks that could be uniting factors, such as a church workday, multiethnic potluck dinners with sharing of cultural distinctives, community service projects (food, housing), alien advisement and counseling, voter registration, other social issues?

C. Linguistic Issues

The Sapir-Whorf hypothesis of social science teaches that our perception of reality is created by the words we use to a large extent. People speaking different languages see things from a different viewpoint. It is to be expected that where more than one language is present, misunderstandings will take place. But the issues for the multicongregation are much larger than that.

Americans are more monolingual than almost any other country in the civilized world. This also affects our other-language tolerance. People in multicongregations can be taught otherwise.

Discuss the following questions and make decisions before conflicts arise.

—What is the major language to be used in the church?

—As already mentioned, in combined services what will be the main language?

—Is it possible to have a running translation of major portions of the service?

—Will the use of separate sections for translation divide rather than unite the church?

—Can some items be done together, such as hymns, prayer, or scripture?

—Are there banners and posters displayed in all languages?

—Would English-speaking people be willing to learn a certain phrase list in the other language(s) for goodwill?

—Could the non-English-language congregation be urged to teach their youth and children to read and write in their own language on a Saturday or some other day?

—Would non-English (whatever is spoken in your ethnic group) as a second language be useful for some of your English-speaking people?

—Are you aware of differences in the number of tones in

the musical scale of your sister congregation? Are there musical chants that are a regular part of their worship experience? Are there songs they prefer rather than the translations of English songs?

D. Organizational Issues

Almost all multicongregations studied in the course of writing this book are led by the English-speaking pastor and controlled by the English-speaking board. An example of local church organization is given in chap. 5. However, certain issues regarding paternalism and American dominance should be discussed. A study of *Missions Have Come Home to America* will also help on this issue.

It will be helpful if the following questions are discussed with the church board and decisions reached in conjunction with the leadership of the ethnic church to be planted.

—Will the membership be combined or listed separately or both?

—Are membership or catechism classes required equally for each new member?

—How are statistics to be reported?

—Will there be a probationary period for certain members, or will it be the same for all?

—How is leadership to be selected for the overall church? Who will vote: the superordinate group or all members? Will the subordinate group have representation on the ruling board? If the pastor is voted on, who can vote?

—Who selects the leadership for the subordinate group? Is the selection made by all groups, or does each group select their own leadership?

—Can members feel free to attend or join another congregation? Will there be bad feelings if a person from the non-English congregation attends the English congregation? Will they be accepted by the English congregation? Will the non-

English-language congregation accuse this one of trying to "act American"?

—Are all groups given equal recognition and status before denominational institutions? Is the superordinate congregation given official status, whereas the others are only unofficially recognized? Is it possible to give separate but equal recognition?

E. Governance Issues

Although closely related to the organizational issues, this opens a new set of concepts.

Discuss some of these:

—Who is the superordinate and who is the subordinate? Do all groups agree to this arrangement? Is this arrangement right? Is equality possible or desirable?

—Who owns the property? Could a "superboard" elected by all the congregations actually hold legal title to all the property?

—How would equal and fair representation on this superboard be assured? Would membership, finances, and building use be deciding items? Would the amount raised by each congregation enter into representation?

—What type of authority would be given to this superboard? Would they govern the finances, the Christian education program, and all other combined activities?

—Will this board meet regularly for prayer and planning?

—Is the arrangement seen as temporary or long-term?

—How are the subordinate group's budgets approved? Are the finances kept separately?

—Do all groups have equal access to the church legal papers, documents, minutes, etc.?

—Does each group pool its finances into the all-church fund? Does each pay a proportion of its gross income into a superboard-managed fund? Or does each subordinate congre-

71

gation pay a portion of its income into the superordinate's account that manages the major facility expenses? Or does each subordinate group pay a set price (like a rental)?

—Who cares for the custodial expenses?

—Who cares for the nursery expenses? Other child care?

—Does each group have legal autonomy? Does each maintain separate bank accounts? Does each have separate IRS designations? Does each group have separate status with the denomination?

F. Self-image Issues

Some of these self-image areas were cared for under the buildings and organizational issues. The decisions made here will largely be reflective of the type of organization you may choose. Either way a new multicongregation should evidence to the community that there is a single unit meeting under one roof. Even if we have organized into various units, it is important that we be viewed as one church. This is our goal.

Consider these issues:

—Will the sign in front of the church reflect equal space for each congregation? Will the congregations be listed alphabetically, according to length in the building, or some other method?

—Is there a common bulletin cover reflecting each pastor equally?

—Is there a common church directory?

—Is a common brochure possible with each congregation given opportunity to list their activities in their own language?

—Is newspaper advertising for all in common?

—Do all groups have equal access to the use of bulletin boards?

G. Theological/Philosophical Issues

Part I of this book is designed to look at culture and how it affects the call God gives us to live in unity one with another. As earlier explained, people grouping is certainly a useful method of evangelism. However, we must not take our eyes off unity, as this will not come naturally. It is not a gift of the Holy Spirit but must be planned. Remember that unity is not sameness. We will never be alike culturally or individually. But God does want us to live in harmony and be one in His Spirit.

To be effective, each congregation must share a common vision.

Discuss these matters:

—Do the groups share a common theological belief?

—Is there a common (written or understood) mission for the groups coming together?

—Is the purpose of the subordinate having separate services to slow down assimilation by the young of their group into the English-speaking group?

—Does a power struggle seem possible in the future? Is one group planning to take over down the line?

—Is the superordinate group inviting other groups in to help with the budget or to promote unity and evangelize the community?

—Will the style of leadership of each group be compatible?

H. Psychological Issues

Most evangelical denominations have not presently developed ways to give ethnic minorities leadership. Those who have pioneered this venture have found that ethnics in leadership are just as effective as their Anglo counterparts. However, it has been proven that both ethnic and Anglo leaders need to guard against a common hazard that can hinder their effectiveness: ethnocentrism.

The answer to the shortage of ethnic leadership is certainly not tokenism. Tokenism only prevents real leadership from developing. Tokenism almost always assures that both sides will not be treated with equality because of giving an unequal loyalty to one side or the other. We are never helped by establishing governmental structures within denominational organizations to create positions for ethnic leaders. However, qualities that are present in individuals should be recognized, whether they are categorized as ethnic or not. It is essential that ethnics surface in positions of leadership.

The issues stated previously should be asked again in light of other matters raised:

—How does each group feel about the other? Do they believe themselves to be of equal or unequal status? Are they partners or master/servant in their relationship?

—Do the groups share similar mutual perceptions of the other? If not, what feedback is in place to correct misconceived or mismatched perceptions?

In order for multicongregations to work, it is important that strong district support be given. A wise district leader can lend credibility to multicongregational efforts. This will encourage the pastor to make it work.

Training is also a key issue. It is vital to a denomination's future that multicongregational pastors be trained. If any denomination sent untrained missionaries overseas, their mission program would be in shambles. Many church leaders feel it is equally essential to educate pastors and Christian workers in the U.S. and Canada on the best methods to offer Christ's love cross-culturally.

4

The Multicongregational Pastor

Many writers have suggested that there are basically three kinds of pastors:

1. The Creator
2. The Organizer
3. The Controller

The **creator** begins with nothing and forms something. It is easy for such a leader to start a group from scratch and attract people and resources from within a targeted area. This entrepreneurial type is often a self-starter who will see remarkable results quickly. However, unless this pastor is surrounded with people who are organizers, his pastorate may be short-lived. But this depends on the church's rate of growth. Usually a change will take place as the group begins to require more time and energy for organization and maintenance.

The **organizer,** on the other hand, is good at taking a parish and organizing it. Many times the creator has left a jumble of pieces behind. The organizer enjoys designing a well-regulated organization and maximizing the resources. The organizer may be tempted to try to do the work of a creator, but seldom will he be successful.

The **controller** finds himself taking an organization and further organizing it. This is often necessary to keep a church going, but it can be simply a frustrated gesture to cover up lack of growth.

Sometimes there is a tendency in large denominations to give too much leadership to controllers and not enough attention to creators. Often educational institutions major their training on the organizer and the controller. These leaders should not be neglected, but it is vital that the creator receive instructions also. Even though certain personality traits are helpful in each of these categories, training is a key feature in effectively planting a church.

In a way distinct from any other church position, the multicongregational pastor has the opportunity to develop all three of these characteristics. Most multicongregations are an outgrowth of an organized congregation that sees their community changing and forms more than one congregation to help meet that need. Therefore, the multicongregational pastor can participate as reorganization takes place simultaneous with church planting. This unique person becomes the catalyst in creating a new model. However, they cannot accomplish it without a trained eye to see the necessary gifts in others that will be active in the model.

Churches in multiethnic neighborhoods will rise or fall on the vision, the skills, the faith, and the integrity of the pastor. To be a pastor is an awesome calling in itself. To be a pastor in a multiethnic situation is an excitement beyond description.

Churches in changing communities need leadership of the finest quality. These people will be both equippers as well as leaders. They will find it necessary to both say, "Charge," to a discouraged congregation and at the same time communicate to their people that such leadership also means, "Follow me."

The pastor of the multicongregation is a specialist. The following traits are essential:

I. A Servant

To the multicongregational pastor, the concept of servanthood takes on a different meaning. Pastoring in a multicultural area magnifies the awareness of social injustice and especially that infamous period of American history when some of our fellow countrymen endured the suffering a pretentious society forced on them. There are so many ugly pictures that servanthood brings to mind. In the secular world many people are engaged as servants of their employer. They are occupied only by the drive to advance in the corporate world. You have probably encountered those who have sold out to a life of crime or live as slaves to a drug habit. Just a little closer home, do I dare mention those who have become enslaved by a well-meaning church? Without realizing it, some dedicated workers have slipped into a life of being pawns of the bureaucratic hierarchy, with no ability to express thought and concern of their own. Then another thought disturbs me. Through the years I have been annoyed by reports of uniformed national servants being summoned by the ringing of a bell in some missionaries' homes. I have served overseas, so I am not confusing adequately paid Christian nationals who help with mission tasks.

As I ponder all these ideas, it is difficult to relate any of them with being a servant in a cross-cultural neighborhood or even to being a slave to Christ. The Bible, however, does emphasize that the disciples received joy as servants of God. Paul speaks to us in Col. 1:24-29:

> Now I rejoice in my sufferings for your sake, and in my flesh I complete what is lacking in Christ's afflictions for the sake of his body, that is, the church, of which I became a minister according to the divine office which was given to me for you, to make the word of God fully known, the mystery hidden for ages and generations but now made manifest to his saints. To them God chose to make known how great among the Gentiles are the riches of the glory of this mystery, which is Christ

in you, the hope of glory. Him we proclaim, warning every man and teaching every man in all wisdom, that we may present every man mature in Christ. For this I toil, striving with all the energy which he mightily inspires within me.

Charles R. Swindoll, in his book *Improving Your Serve,* points to some biblical definitions of servanthood. They include:

a. Transparent Humanity (1 Cor. 2:1-3; 2 Cor. 10:10). Servants have needs and admit them. They do not have all of life wired perfectly, and they don't hide that fact. They are human (with all its flaws) and openly declare it.

b. Genuine Humility (1 Cor. 2:4-5). Image-conscious leaders exalt themselves. Servant-conscious disciples exalt Christ.

c. Absolute Honesty (2 Cor. 4:1-2; 1 Thess. 2:3-4). Integrity is beautiful and refreshing. To rid one's life of hypocrisy, political games, and human manipulation is real and genuine. Christ is bound to shine through.

d. Unselfishness (Gen. 2:25—3:13; Matt. 20:25-28; Phil. 2:3-5). The pronoun *I* is capitalized only in the English language. This may reflect the superior feelings we have in our culture for the individual. Many cultures feel and think collectively. The feeling of superiority has helped Americans place their products at the top around the world. However, we have often alienated ourselves from others by not accepting them for who they are.

Dr. Swindoll points to the Beatitudes as a genuine guideline for servanthood.[1]

Although these thoughts are excellent guidelines for all pastors, they become essential in dealing in cross-cultural church planting.

2. Change Agent

The pastor of a church in Los Angeles shared this story: His church was more than 50 years old. In the 1930s the racial and socioeconomic profile of the church and its neighborhood were the same. Today the neighborhood is 60 percent Asian, from various ethnic and language backgrounds. Another 20 percent speak only Spanish. Even the Anglos that remain have seen a drastic shift in socioeconomic status. The pastor exclaimed, "We have the same basic program that we had 50 years ago, and that program is not meeting the needs of our neighborhood. I know that we need to change; but how do we go about it?"

Kert Lewin, a leading authority on social change, wrote that a successful effort to change involves three steps:

    a. Unfreeze the present situation.
    b. Move the group to a new level.
    c. Refreeze the group life at the new level.[2]

One of the major tasks of the multicongregational pastor is to awaken the church to the change taking place in the community. Many times these significant changes have occurred so slowly that the church membership has been unaware. The methods involved in unfreezing the situation must be developed surrounding the needs of each church. They may include (1) biblical preaching using examples of multifaceted ministry that are pointed out in the introduction to Part II, (2) displaying facts concerning the community either in a multimedia presentation or attractive handouts, (3) bringing in an outside consultant from your denomination or a nearby college, or another multicongregational pastor whose church is successful, (4) sponsoring a field trip into the community for leaders to explore and discover the facts of change for themselves, (5) a retreat where each person has an opportunity to express his feelings, to study the Word, and to discover the opportunities God has given to your church.

According to Fritz Kunkel, no one makes any significant change until they are motivated by pain.[3] Usually a church will be best motivated toward change as they realize impending crisis in their existence or have their eyes opened to surrounding external forces that threaten their security.

The planning process described in Chapter 1 of Part 2 is necessary, whether conducted formally or informally by the multicongregational pastor. This will begin a church in the journey of moving to a new level of ministry. A church that is challenged by its pastor will begin to move out into its community. But to do this, a feasibility study showing the pressing needs of the people of that community is often necessary. Specific programs must be designed to meet the local needs. When this is accomplished, a church moves beyond the unfreezing of their status quo and into a new dimension of exciting ministry.

Since there is a tendency for a church to slip back to an old level of existence, it is essential that the multicongregational pastor see as his task the stabilizing of the church at the new level of ministry.

C. Peter Wagner points out that it is the pastor's role to change the understanding in the communication system used by the church. Every church has a medium established in which to communicate that message. The objective is to have the information received by the audience.

MESSAGE ⟶ MEDIUM ⟶ AUDIENCE

However, when the audience changes, there are several choices a congregation must make.

(1) The congregation can leave the message alone and also stick to the same methods (medium). The result is that they miss the audience.

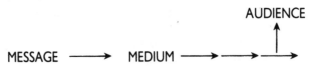

(2) The congregation could choose to change the message and therefore better hit the audience.

(3) It is the responsibility of the multicongregational pastor to help his congregation see the importance of changing their methods (medium) in order to communicate with the changing audience.

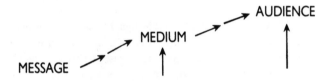

It is never acceptable to change the message we preach. But the methods can easily be adjusted to better meet the need of a targeted group.

3. Cross-cultural Attitudes

Much like plants that lean toward the sun, you reflect your attitudes toward people and circumstances by the direction in which you lean. It is true that each person is personally influenced by past experiences. The way we were educated combines to develop our thought patterns for ministry.

There are times when it is necessary for a person to purposefully redirect crucial attitudes to adjust to the ministry area to which God has called them.

Some of the key attitudes for a multicongregational pastor are:

a. **Change.** One characteristic of cross-cultural thought structure that seems to be constant is change. It is everywhere: politics, business dealings, community life, cultural life, ethical concerns. Although change is a part of everyone's life, change among multicultural and multilingual groups within Canada and the United States is most frequent.

How should the pastor and people in this setting react? In comparison with churches in cross-cultural neighborhoods, other congregations usually offer the security of a relatively slow turnover in their church and minimal community transition. A cross-cultural neighborhood, on the other hand, offers the stress of rapid transposition and the possibility of regular spiritual renewal.

It is common to avoid change because often we feel threatened. The new is unpredictable, and it requires extra energy to adapt. It challenges our present way of life; therefore, we can experience strong emotions, such as fear or anger.

Life without change is not necessarily a life of security. Change quite often is beneficial. God is unchanging, but He is a God of change. This is evident in His handiwork all around us, for He has allowed many of His creations to evolve into something even more beautiful. Consider for a moment the butterfly. Its beauty depicts the artistry of God. As we watch it gracefully flutter from flower to flower, we hardly remember it was once a crawling caterpillar limited by physical boundaries. Yet, because it was willing to submit to nature's laws, it can now soar to places it only once dreamed. Change many times brings freedom.

The best example is the conversion of a sinner and the change that comes into a life that experiences the infilling of the Holy Spirit. God is in the process of changing everything from what it is to what it ought to be.

Just as we can change and be the agents that oversee the change process, so we can accept change as an acceptable way of life. By this we can allow the Holy Spirit to unleash our creative energies. We become God's agent for the present and the future instead of being tied only to the past. Through this spirit of obedience God will work to bring a fresh spiritual power to our life.

b. **Property.** Often when a young couple marries, they begin to plan for the time they will be able to purchase a home. Our culture has taught us the value of owning a piece of property, one of the great dreams still prevalent in Canada and the United States.

A pastor's outlook concerning the total facility will greatly affect how the congregation responds to transition. The buildings and property must be seen not as an economic investment but as a place for worship and ministry to people. Who does own the church? A minister must find the answer to this question before he begins a journey into multicongregational work. Is the church owned by the heavy tithers who regularly invest in God's work? Is it those who have developed a squatter's rights attitude by possessing the land years ago? Or could it be the pastoral staff?

It is natural that a person feel ownership toward property that has his own name on the deed. However, members of a congregation where the property deed has the church's name listed should view the buildings and land as God's. *It is all His!*

When the undershepherd instills into his people a high sense of the value of individuals, there is a greater loss felt when someone dies without Christ than if some damage occurs to the property. The Bible teaches us that just one soul is worth more than the world.

Buildings are a necessity. It is not suggested that we meet in tents or under a shade tree. But having the right attitude is vital in order for a cross-cultural pastor to guide his flock to place a higher value on people rather than on property. If property is more precious than people, there will be no problem selling the church to the highest bidder, then moving to the suburbs and forgetting about the spiritual needs of the people back in the old neighborhood. A correct belief concerning property includes God as the Owner, church people as the lessor, and the buildings as a place of ministry. This position is necessary in order to release our facilities for multicongregational use by several ministry groups.

   c. **People.** It is imperative for the multicongregational pastor to evaluate personal feelings toward the worth of others. What are our criteria for judging human worth? Culture often influences us to judge others on their outward appearance, material resources, positions of status, and business success. In our society nonaffluent, nonmale, nonwhite, unbeautiful, uneducated, unyoung, and unwealthy people are seen with less respect. There must be no room in the pastor's heart for any of these prejudices. The successful planting of a multicongregation will hinge on the leader's attitude.

   People quickly understand a church's attitude toward them. Does the local church always overlook nonwhites for positions of leadership? Are refugees given leftover materials, space, schedules, and budgets after other needs are met? Do people refer to "us" and "them" when they speak of people who are not quite "like us"?

   To guide the feelings of people in the congregation, prayerfully speak on James 2. However, the congregation will observe the actions of their minister. This will influence them more than any sermon.

   Personal attitudes surely affect God's mission in a neighborhood. The reflection of ourselves must be a constant reminder that God is remolding us into what He wants us to be. Even when it is tough, our attitudes must mirror those of

Jesus in order to draw others toward the Savior. As missionaries, we will welcome change and take up the challenge of guiding others though the transition necessary to be effective in our part of the world.

4. Ability to Live with Compromise

There is a constant necessity to settle for what might appear to be second-best in a multicongregational ministry. This is not negative, for it has brought creativity to the surface in more than one pastor's mind. A host of things can affect a plan set out by a well-meaning pastor. Pluralism of the congregation, the lack of money for funding, the absence of sufficient workers, or any of a multitude of other reasons might force a pastor to settle gratefully for a foot instead of a mile. Most of the compromise is necessary because the pastor is more aware of the circumstances and has a broader vision for the whole program. This can be very frustrating for the energetic pastor who must take time to educate the church and wait for them to develop a more supportive role.

The multiethnic community is bulging with needs. It is essential that the pastor and people have a vision of how they can help the local needy. However, it is necessary for them to evaluate what can be done with the present resources and decide how much can be accomplished at this time. Today, you may not view this as compromise. At some time when you are disappointed over a program that has to be put on the shelf, be realistic and remember that this is not uncommon when working in a multilingual church.

5. Criticism and Rejection

The multicongregation is not a common model in many areas of Canada and the United States. It is possible that it will not be totally supported by some leadership. You may even be considered a radical by others who are more traditionalists.

But your greatest concern will be the division that can occur within a congregation that is trying to reach out cross-culturally. Because the church people are from different backgrounds, they will observe this type of outreach from a variety of opinions. In even the best of circumstances, the pastor is often found to be the lightning rod for ideological, political, social, cultural, and even geographical differences that may be in a church body. But in a multicongregation where the differences between people are greater than average, the pastor must be prepared to receive some criticism and even rejection without being personally offended.

A leader should always keep an open mind and let people with disagreements be heard. Listening and explaining will many times settle disputes, for often the lack of information is the basic source for difficulty. Neither the church nor the pastor can ever be all things to all people. But it is important to try to preserve peace. God desires unity, and He will help you.

6. A Sense of Humor

Respect the assignment God has given you, but do not take yourself too seriously. If you cannot laugh at many of the everyday circumstances, you will have nothing left to do but cry. Recognizing your own limitations, both personally and in your field of labor, will allow you to see humor in things that you cannot solve. Laughter is therapeutic. Use it often.

Conclusion

Today, North Americans are losing touch with one another. The motivation to help, encourage, and serve other individuals is vanishing. Yet it is through these services that happiness and peaceful fulfillment are found. A Christian is responsible to perform as a servant and be an example to inspire others in a life of service.

God is committed to one major objective concerning our

lives: to conform us "to the image of his Son" (Rom. 8:29). Mark 10:45 says of Him, "For the Son of man also came not to be served but to serve, and to give his life as a ransom for many." So it is easy to conclude that He did come both to serve and to train us to be servers and givers of ourselves.

Pastors must always see themselves as having a dual role. They are called out of an unholy world to a life of holiness and to be possessed by God. But they must realize they are being sent back into the world to witness and to serve. Many times churches have been unable to emphasize both of these at the same time. In an emphasis of holiness, ministers have often wrongly drawn away from the sinful world and its needs. At other times, while immersed in the life of the world, they have assimilated the world's standards and values. There must be a balance.

Creative and innovative pastors will find it is essential to take a fresh approach to this dual role. The church needs the minister, and the minister needs the church.

You will appreciate these words of an old, wise professor: "There is a new problem in our country. We are becoming a nation that is dominated by large institutions—churches, businesses, governments, labor unions, universities—and these big institutions are not serving us well. I hope that all of you will be concerned about this. Now you can do as I do, stand outside and criticize, bring pressure if you can, write and argue about it. All this may do some good. But, nothing of substance will happen unless there are people inside institutions who are able to (and want to) lead them into better performance for the public good. Some of you ought to make careers inside these big institutions and become a force for good—from the inside."[4]

Only time will tell the effect that the multicongregational model will have on the total church and its ability to reach the multicultural and multilingual groups of Canada and the

United States. But the outcome will greatly depend upon the pastor's willingness to live a life of servanthood with Jesus as an example.

1. Charles R. Swindoll, *Improving Your Serve: The Art of Unselfish Living* (Waco, Tex.: Word Books, Publisher, 1981), 23-37.

2. Kert Lewin, "Frontiers in Group Dynamics," *Human Relations* 1 (1947): 13-40.

3. Cecil Osborne, *The Art of Understanding Yourself* (Grand Rapids: Zondervan Publishing House, 1967), 20.

4. Robert K. Greenleaf, *Servant Leadership* (New York: Paulist Press, 1977), 1-2.

5

How the Nazarenes Have Responded

The ecclesiastical structure of the Church of the Nazarene is similar to many other American Protestant denominations. From its beginnings in Los Angeles in 1895 it quickly evolved into a nationwide organization and soon was deploying missionaries overseas.

At the very beginning provision was made for a general church hierarchy with the naming of general superintendents as overseers of the total church operation. Patterning the organization after the Methodist church, from which many of the early leaders and pastors came, a district level of organization was set in place under which local churches were given direction and expected to function in harmony with the general and district Church of the Nazarene.

The form of government in the Church of the Nazarene is best described as a combination of congregational and episcopal structures.

Local churches call their own pastors with the approval of the district superintendent. District superintendents give guidance to the churches under their supervision in accordance with the policies established by the general church. The general superintendents are elected by a General Assembly made up of delegates from the local churches.

Accountability lines are clearly drawn and provisions made for checks and balances within the total system.

It is presently the intent and direction of this denomination to become an international church in every way possible. This means representation at the general church level is beginning to be a reflection of the multicultural and multilingual world of the 20th century. General church leadership at the highest level in the Church of the Nazarene is still nearly all white-Anglo, but representation on the General Board and delegates to the General Assembly reflect the ethnic/language mix of the Church of the Nazarene.

At the district level the leadership continues to be white-Anglo in most instances. However, ethnic/language coordinators and assistants are appearing in a growing number of district organizations as awareness of the changing cultural communities grows.

It is on the local church level that the most rapid and dramatic change is taking place. Out of the crucible of direct contact with the "stewpot" atmosphere of urban communities, the local congregations and pastors are pouring their ministries into new forms fashioned to meet the pressing need to minister to the mission field on their doorstep. This field is in the form of ethnic/language people groups surrounding their parish centers.

Prior to 1980 most Nazarene churches and districts were dealing with the multicultural neighborhood independent of one another.

In response to inquiries and suggestions from pastors and district leadership in the Hawaii Pacific and Los Angeles districts, General Superintendent Dr. V. H. Lewis opened the door to the process that led to the formation of a Multicongregational Commission. A report was presented to the 1985 General Assembly and subsequently adopted.

This led to changes in the official *Manual of the Church of the Nazarene* allowing for structures to be formed for the development and recognition of the multicongregational church.

THE REPORT OF THE MULTICONGREGATION CHURCHES COMMISSION

to the 21st General Assembly of the Church of the Nazarene
June 1985 at Anaheim, Calif.

[The bracketed portions are more recent interpolations.]

Members of the Commission:

Paul Benefiel, *chairman;* Jerry Appleby, *secretary;* Habib Alajaji, Yoon K. Chun, Dallas Mucci, Jonathan Salgado, Charles Thompson, Jerry White; and Glen Van Dyne, *editor*

The United States and Canada experienced dramatic changes in the middle and late 1800s through immigrants from Europe seeking new opportunities. Now, in the latter part of the 20th century amidst the hi-tech revolution, immigration from the developing countries and the Orient has increased dramatically. This has created significant changes, particularly in the large urban centers.

A statistical study shows that in 140 years (from 1820 to 1957) there was a total of 35 million immigrants to the USA. From 1971 to 1980 there were nearly 4 million immigrants . . . 97% of the first 140 years of immigrants were Anglos, but only 24% of those immigrating in the 1970s were Anglos, 41% were Latin Americans and 32% Asians and 3% others. The same study shows 1.1 million newcomers each year in the United States. 400,000 of these are legal immigrants, 600,000 are undocumented. 100,000 are refugees and special immigrants.

From its inception the Church of the Nazarene has recognized the opportunity to minister to these immigrant groups. Dr. Bresee had both Spanish and Chinese language works in the original First Church of the Nazarene in Los Angeles, making it a multicongregational church.

Today, the most conservative statistics we have indicate there has been tremendous growth in the number of multicongregational churches since 1970. The number of U.S. and Canadian multicongregational churches has grown from 1 in 1976 to 22 in 1980 and to 121 in 1984. This is a 2200% increase from 1976 to 1980 and a 600% increase from 1981 to 1984. If this growth pattern continues, by 1990 at least 30% of our U.S. and Canadian churches will be multicongregational. Of the 450 ethnic works in existence in 1983 (either fully organized churches or church-type missions) nearly 60% of them meet in multicongregational church settings.

The total number of ethnic works has increased from 36 in 1940 to 499 in 1985 with 300 of these coming to fully organized status. Much of this growth has occurred due to organized churches being willing to share their facilities with other cultural groups. This has resulted in better stewardship of buildings and a more rapid carrying out of the "Great Commission." . . .

As regular districts have responded to evangelizing the ethnic groups around them, there has been tremendous growth. This growth has accelerated as the multicongregational model has been used.

Two examples of multicongregational models are:

1. More than one organized church meeting in the same building

All congregations work in a continuing fellowship to build unity. All expenses associated with the use of the building facilities are shared proportionately by each group. Each group is accountable to the district superintendent.

2. More than one cultural group in one church organization

This includes several congregations in one church organization, or, it could be several language classes meeting separately yet all part of one organization. Each group or class has its own leader. Where possible, ethnic leadership is desirable.

The local church sponsors these classes or groups and supports them financially. The group is accountable to the pastoral administrator and local church board. Church board committees have the responsibilities of developing programs. These groups may or may not become fully organized churches. However, they may come into membership of the sponsoring organized local church.

[We believe that the church has a responsibility of reaching these people with the gospel. It seems to us that in the providence of God this country among all the other countries has opened its doors for the immigrants because of the freedom we have in preaching the gospel and evangelizing in the name of Jesus Christ. This is our golden opportunity to reach the multitudes. Therefore, we need to have specific guidelines and regulations to be of help to those churches who have already started to meet the challenge with multi-congregational ministries and to others who want to do so in the future.

[POTENTIAL FOR FUTURE ETHNIC MINISTRIES:

[Within the Church of the Nazarene the multicongregational church has emerged as one of the most productive ways to develop work among the many ethnic groups in the United States. As indicated before, the number of reported multicongregations between 1976 and 1984 increased from 1 to 121. This dramatic increase in multicongregational churches indicates the possibilities for development of such ministries.]

The reasons for the development of such churches are:

I. THE SCRIPTURAL MANDATE:
   A. The fulfillment of the Great Commission begins at home (Acts 1:8).
   B. Jesus prayed for the unity of the Church (John 17:20-23).

II. CHURCH GROWTH FACTORS:
   A. The formation of a new congregation is linked to an established church.
   B. The mother church is better able to nurture and develop the new congregation.
   C. The awareness of "mission" is fostered in the established church.

III. ECONOMIC FACTORS:
   A. It is good stewardship of building and property dollars to use the facilities for more than one congregation.
   B. The daughter church (ofttimes from a lower income level) is assisted in its development without heavy financial strain.

IV. THE IMMEDIACY OF THE NEED:
   A. People who have recently been uprooted from their cultural setting are very receptive to the gospel.
   B. To wait until we can reach as many of these groups by traditional means may be too late.

93

As the Church of the Nazarene looks into the future, there is a growing awareness of the need to impact the cities of the world and a burden to reach out across racial, ethnic, and cultural boundaries with the gospel of Jesus Christ. To accomplish this mission the church will need to use every vehicle available to it. The multicongregational church is one such vehicle.

To illustrate the potential for multicongregational churches consider the Hispanic population of the United States. There are 298 counties with 2,500 or more Hispanics in which we have one or more Anglo churches but no Hispanic congregation. [At present we have 196 Hispanic congregations in America (125 fully organized churches, 54 church-type missions, and 17 language Bible classes).] If the churches in each of these counties would target an area in which to organize one new Hispanic congregation, we could increase our Hispanic language congregations by 173%.

[Obviously that many new Hispanic works could not be organized at one time, because of the limitation of workers, etc. However,] when we see the potential for growth among the Blacks, Koreans, Hispanics, Armenians, Filipinos, Chinese, Cambodians, and other ethnic groups, the possibilities for organizing new areas of ministry develop in an astonishing way. We are reminded again of the words of the founder of the Church of the Nazarene, Dr. Phineas F. Bresee, "We are debtors to give the gospel to every creature in the same measure that we have received it."

[As a result of the adoption of the Multicongregational Commission Report, the following paragraphs were added to the *Manual of the Church of the Nazarene* (1985 edition) under the chapter heading: THE LOCAL CHURCH.]

100.1. *The Multicongregational Church.* Organized local churches may enlarge their ministry by establishing Bible classes in various languages using the facilities of these churches. These Bible classes may develop into church-type missions or fully organized churches [100]. This may result in more than one congregation existing in the same building, with the approval of the district superintendent. In such multicongregational churches where not all the individual congregations are fully organized churches, the District Advisory Board, with the approval of the district superintendent and the general superintendent in jurisdiction, may grant to such congregations the rights and privileges of an organized local church subject to the following conditions:

1. Such congregations may not be incorporated separate from the organized local church.

2. Such congregations shall not hold title to property separate from the organized local church.

3. Such congregations shall not incur indebtedness without the approval of the district superintendent, the church board of the organized local church, and the District Advisory Board.

4. No such congregation may withdraw as a body from the organized local church or in any way sever its relation thereto except by the express permission of the district superintendent in consultation with the pastor of the local church.

102.5. In multicongregational churches, where more than one organized church shares the same facility, incorporation may take place in partnership where local laws allow.

106.4. Churches may be declared inactive for a period of transition by action of the Board of General Superintendents on the recommendation of the District Advisory Board.

An Example of a Multicongregational Church of the Nazarene

To see just how this concept adopted by the General Assembly works out in the field, we need to look at a specific example. The one chosen here is the oldest and most fully developed.

Los Angeles First Church of the Nazarene (founded in 1895) was actually a multicongregational church at the turn of the century. However, it did not have an official charter as a multicongregational church until 1989.

The process of arriving at the present charter was a six-year journey that led them through many stages and not a few experiments along the way. Pastor Ron Benefiel has directed this process and serves as senior pastor and administrative pastor of this multicongregational church, which is made up of English, Korean, Filipino, and Spanish congregations.

If this were not enough going on in one building, consider that there is also a Spanish Bible School (Instituto Teologico Nazareno), a graduate school of urban ministry studies (Bresee Institute), a preschool, elementary school, after-school program, and various social service programs for the homeless and low-income people who live in the community.

In addition, this multicongregational church has sponsored new outreach works in Hollywood, Exposition Park, and Central City areas of Greater Los Angeles. To use the term *multi-* in relationship to this local church is a gross understatement.

MULTICONGREGATIONAL STRUCTURE FOR FIRST CHURCH OF THE NAZARENE
Los Angeles, Calif.

PREAMBLE

We believe:

A. God has called us as a church to minister to our community.

1. As a church, we have a permanent ongoing commitment to reach the people groups to Mid-Wilshire Los Angeles.

2. Our intention is to develop and maintain ministries to our community that respond to the ever-changing demographics, socioeconomics, and human and spiritual needs represented by the people of our community.

B. God has called us to minister together as one church with multiple congregations and ministries.

1. We believe that our spiritual union in the Body of Christ should be appropriately reflected in our organizational structures.

2. We believe that the ministry of our church is strengthened by being one church with a shared calling and vision of ministry to our community.

3. We believe one of the great resources God has given us for ministry is our facility, and it is our responsibility as good stewards of God's resource to both maintain it adequately and use it to its full potential.

C. All members of the various congregations of First Church of the Nazarene, Los Angeles, Calif., have equal standing.

1. The church facilities are jointly owned by the membership of the congregations of the church.

2. The membership of the congregations of the church has a shared responsibility for determining policy regarding facilities, equipment, and joint programming.

3. The membership of the congregations of the church has a shared financial responsibility for maintaining facilities and supporting joint programs.

I. Authority of Individual Congregations

A multicongregational organizational structure that implements the above statement of beliefs necessarily includes the formation of a governing board (Multicongregational Council) with authority over each of the congregations and ministries of the church in specific areas. However, the authority of the council over each of the congregations is limited in its scope to matters that are either necessary to the efficient functioning of the whole church or mutually agreed upon. For example:

A. Each congregation that has been granted all the rights and privileges of a fully organized church by the District Advisory Board has complete autonomous authority in the pastoral selection process as specified for a local congregation in the *Manual of the Church of the Nazarene.*

B. Each congregation is responsible and accountable for its own financial budgeting, collection of tithes and offerings, bookkeeping, and payment of financial obligations including all district, education, and general budgets.

C. Each congregation has authority for development of in-congregation church programming (e.g., worship services, Sunday School, outreach ministries, youth programming, etc.) as facility space is available.

D. Each congregation, with the approval of the Multicongregational Council, may take responsibility for the purchase of real estate, vehicles, and equipment. (See IV-A.)

II. Authority of the Multicongregational Council

The authority of the Multicongregational Council shall include, but not be limited to, the following:

A. PROPERTY. This includes purchase of property, oversight of building maintenance and repairs, purchase, maintenance and use supervision of corporately owned equipment, and scheduling of the use of church facilities. Corporately owned equipment could include, but is not limited to, office equipment, audiovisual equipment, vehicles, kitchen equipment, recreational equipment, educational aids, etc.

B. JOINT PROGRAMMING. This includes the planning and implementation of multicongregational services, meetings, recreational activities, outreach ministries, and social activities as useful in accomplishing the overall mission of the church.

C. STAFF. This includes the responsibility for hiring, creating job descriptions, and supervising custodial personnel and the all-church receptionist, as well as any other all-church staff.

D. POLICIES. This includes establishing and maintaining guidelines for daily operations of the church, setting insurance liability minimums, and designating other legal requirements for any operation, activity, or action of the church and all of its ministries and congregations.

E. FINANCIAL MATTERS. The Multicongregational Council will have a separate operating budget, which will include purchases, maintenance, repair, and supply expenses related to the building, facilities, real property, and corporately owned equipment. Also included are utilities, compensation to custodial, reception, and other all-church personnel, and any other obligations that are jointly incurred by all congregations or are the joint responsibility of the congregations of the First Church of the Nazarene of Los Angeles, Calif.

III. Multicongregational Council Membership and Finances

A. The council shall consist of a minimum of 12 voting members. The council shall designate in its final meeting of the year the size of the council for the coming year. This shall be determined by a simple majority vote. If no vote is taken, the number of council members will remain the same for the coming year.

B. In the event a congregation achieves full congregational status midyear, it will seat one voting lay member on the council and the pastor, who will have privileges of the floor without a vote, for the duration of the fiscal year.

C. The averaged sum of the percentages of the statistical index and financial strength of each congregation with full congregational status in proportion to the averaged sum of the percentages of the statistical index and financial strength of all congregations with full congregational status shall determine the proportionate council membership from each congregation. (See chart on page 103.)

D. As long as there are at least three congregations with full congregational status, no one congregation may seat more than 50 percent of the voting members of the council.

E. Election of members to the Multicongregational Council shall take place at each congregation's annual meeting. The church board of a given congregation may elect a replacement member for one of its congregation's council members who resigns midyear.

F. One-third of the financial responsibility of each congregation will be based on the previous year's statistical index and two-thirds of the previous year's financial index. The financial index of each congregation shall be derived from the annual total receipts of tithes and offerings. In determining a congregation's financial index, grants, endowments, nonbudgeted facility improvement contributions, and the amount paid on all district, educational, and general budgets are to be excluded. The statistical index is to be derived by totaling the sum of the previous year's average Sunday morning worship attendance plus the number of members in the congregational report at the previous year-end. Each congregation's specific requirements for membership must be submitted to the council for approval (see chart on page 103 for an example of the process of determining the number of council members and financial responsibilities for each congregation).

G. Each congregation with full congregational status will have a minimum of one vote on the council. The pastor of a congregation shall automatically serve as the second regular voting representative to the council from that congregation. In the case in which a congregation is allowed only one representative, that representative must be a layperson, and the pastor becomes a nonvoting member of the council with floor privileges but no voting privilege.

H. Ministries of a congregation or of the church as a whole that have facility needs above and beyond normal congregational use (e.g., Mid-Wilshire Christian School, Instituto Teologico Nazareno, Bresee Institute) and congregations without full congregational status are to be considered separately with regard to financial obligations for facility use. Facility repairs and maintenance relating to such ministries will be the responsibility of the council. Each of these ministries' share of facility-use expenses will be annually determined by the council with consideration given to its overall use of the facility. The council may designate representation of such ministries on the council where appropriate.

I. The council shall elect officers and appoint committees as necessary to carry out its assigned responsibilities (e.g., secretary, treasurer, Property Committee, Finance and Legal Issues Committee).

J. To determine the chairperson of the council, a nominating committee of laypersons chaired by the council secretary and including the council treasurer, council subcommittee chairpersons, and one additional lay representative from each congregation with full congregational status shall place one name into nomination to the council for election. The nomination of the chairperson must be approved by the district superintendent before the council vote. The candidate must be senior pastor of one of the congregations with full congregational status. In order to elect, the council must approve the candidate by a simple majority vote. The chairperson will serve for a period of two years. Additionally, the chairperson will serve a concurrent two-year period as administrative pastor and president of First Church of the Nazarene of Los Angeles, Calif. There is no limit to the number of terms that an administrative pastor may serve.

K. The council shall appoint a committee to prepare a budget for each fiscal year. The budget must be approved by the council.

L. Any facility renovation, improvements, or other nonbudgeted expense items proposed by a congregation are to be referred to the council. Any such items approved by the council are the financial obligation of the congregations whose boards vote to participate in the project. With the approval of the council and the affirmative vote of the board of each congregation with full congregational status, a project may be taken on by the church as a whole and paid for out of the council budget. If the project requires the borrowing of funds, affirmative votes from the membership of each congregation or of a combined meeting of members of all congregations must be obtained.

IV. Legal Issues

A. For legal purposes the council shall serve as the church board of First Church of the Nazarene, Los Angeles, Calif. Ownership of all real estate, vehicles, and equipment will legally lie with First Church of the Nazarene, Los Angeles, Calif. However, with the consent of the council a congregation may assume financial and administrative responsibility for property, vehicles, or equipment.

B. No portion of the church facility or property at 3401 West Third Street, Los Angeles, or other jointly owned properties may be sold or otherwise disposed of without the approval of the council, two-thirds vote of the members present and voting at a duly called meeting of the combined congregations with full congregational status, the District Church Properties Board, and the District Advisory Board.

C. The *Manual of the Church of the Nazarene* shall serve as the bylaws of the organization.

V. Congregational Status

A. A congregation may be considered for full congregational status if:

1. It is recognized by the district as a church-type mission or fully organized church;

2. The pastor has a district minister's license or is an ordained elder in the Church of the Nazarene; and

3. It qualifies for at least one representative to join the council (.50 from the formula). This requirement may be waived by a two-thirds vote of the council.

101

Full congregational status may then be granted upon the simple majority vote of the council with the approval of the district superintendent.

B. For a congregation to maintain full congregational status, it must:

1. Follow the doctrinal guidelines of the *Manual of the Church of the Nazarene* and distribute the doctrinal belief statement to the congregation annually as outlined in the *Manual;*

2. Remain current on all multicongregational financial responsibilities;

3. Maintain at least an annual 67% attendance record at council meetings; and

4. Participate regularly in the joint programs, meetings, services, or other events of the church.

A congregation that fails to meet the requirements for maintaining full congregational status may be reinstated by a simple majority vote of the council members from congregations maintaining full congregational status. If such a congregation is not reinstated, it may continue as a department or ministry of the church and comes under the supervision of the council.

C. With the affirmative vote of any two congregational boards with full congregational status, the two-thirds majority vote of the council members (excluding members from the congregation in question), and the approval of the District Advisory Board, the status of a congregation with full congregational status may be changed to that of a department or ministry of the church. Such a congregation may be granted the privilege of the floor at council meetings but would not have voting privileges.

D. A congregation without full congregational status may be requested to relocate upon a simple majority vote of the council and approval of the District Advisory Board.

E. With a simple majority vote of a congregation and approval of the District Advisory Board, a congregation may withdraw its affiliation with the church. It is understood that such a congregation has no equity in the church facility. Bank accounts, property, and vehicles to which it has been given rights of ownership by authorization of the council will be retained by the withdrawing congregation.

EXAMPLE of determination of proportionate council membership and corresponding financial responsibility of each congregation:

	Financial Strength	% of Total	Average Morning Worship Attend.	Plus Membership		Equals Statistical Index		% of Total
English	$150,000	60%	275	+	300	=	575	44%
Spanish	66,000	26%	250	+	200	=	450	35%
Korean	22,000	9%	100	+	135	=	235	18%
Filipino	12,000	5%	25	+	15	=	40	3%
TOTAL	$250,000	100%					1,300	100%

% Financial Strength Plus Statistical Index Divided by 2 equals Proportionate Representation and Financial Responsibility

English	60% +	44%	divided by	2 =	52.0%
Spanish	26% +	35%	divided by	2 =	30.5%
Korean	9% +	18%	divided by	2 =	13.5%
Filipino	5% +	3%	divided by	2 =	4.0%
					100.0%

In this example, if the council base was 12 members, 6 would be from the English-speaking congregation, 4 would be from the Spanish-speaking congregation, 2 from the Korean congregation, and the necessary 1 from the Filipino congregation.

VI. Charter Amendments

A. This charter may be amended upon simple majority vote of three-fourths of the congregational boards of congregations with full congregational status and two-thirds vote of the council.

April 10, 1989

The District Structure and Multicongregational Churches

Caught in the middle, so to speak, of this developing wave of multicongregational churches is the district structure. Depending on the specific district, leadership is either leading the way or responding to the grass roots movement as local churches become concerned and respond to the culturally changing communities where they are located.

Concerns and questions being addressed at the district level in the Church of the Nazarene include these:

1. When several local churches develop multicongregational ministries, there arises a need for coordination and ethnic/language (E/L)-oriented activities.

2. The need arises to determine how E/L coordinators relate to the district leadership.

3. Close interaction between E/L and sponsoring pastors tend to emphasize personality differences. These differences become more critical when pastoral changes take place.

4. The multicongregational factor becomes critical in the selection of pastors of sponsoring churches.

5. The same processes that take place at the local level must be addressed at the district level.

6. Provision for cultural interaction appears to be a priority at the district level.

7. Training of leadership and raising the level of awareness among the membership needs to be addressed. This re-

sponsibility may need to be shared with the general church level of leadership.

8. Recognition, licensing, and credentialing of multicultural and urban pastoral leadership is a concern for both district and general level of the denomination.

It is clear to those involved in multicongregational churches in the Church of the Nazarene that much remains to be done to bring this needed concept to reality on a broader scale. But the stewpot is beginning to boil, and the aroma is appetizing.

6

Dividends for Those Who Try

It is tragic that so much of our society is divided along racial, ethnic, and cultural lines. In the secular world, where greed and hate are often the motivating factors, we are not surprised when this is true. But it saddens us when God's people are separated by these same lines. It is startling and embarrassing to admit, but the world is ahead of the Church in taking steps to mend these issues.

Unhealthy division within the church becomes a lethal weapon for the devil. It not only will damage those within the circle of the church family but also will spill over into the community, spreading hatred like a contagious disease. Christianity cannot tolerate this, for we must be united in one spirit as children of God. In John 17:21 Jesus prayed that all believers might be one in order to overcome the world.

God does not require that all churches be integrated. But there are benefits for those churches willing to function harmoniously as the Body of Christ. There are also compensations for the church that accentuates their unity in Christ while acknowledging each individual culture. These dividends are felt collectively within the church as well as individually.

A. Biblical Promises of Dividends

Second Cor. 9:6-13 illustrates the rewards of giving ourselves to the cause of sowing and reaping. There are four promises given to the faithful:

1. The reward will be personal (vv. 6-8). "Every blessing" is promised to those who sow bountifully. But they will also have "enough of everything" and so may provide abundantly "for every good work."

2. The reward will be to the nations of the world (v. 9). "As it is written, 'He scatters abroad, he gives to the poor; his righteousness endures for ever.'" The *ethnē* (meaning "nations" in Greek) will hear according to the amount of seeds we sow.

3. The reward will be to an individual or church body that is faithful (vv. 10-11). God is the One who "will supply and multiply your resources and increase the harvest of your righteousness." Even the seed that you sow will be increased, and in that sense "you will be enriched in every way for great generosity."

4. The reward will be the expression of praise to God by many people (vv. 12-13). "For the rendering of this service not only supplies the wants of the saints but also overflows in many thanksgivings to God. Under the test of this service, you will glorify God by your obedience in acknowledging the gospel of Christ, and by the generosity of your contribution for them and for all others."

B. Other Dividends

God in His love cares deeply for each individual's body, soul, mind, spirit, and social relationships. He calls those of us who have trusted Christ His children without regard to our racial or national background. How amazing that God in His infinite wisdom has chosen to use us as instruments to reach the rest of mankind, who are lost. There are a series of benefits for those who choose the multicongregational approach in reaching cross-culturally. Among them are:

1. THE SOCIAL DIVIDEND:
The Reward of Appreciating the Cultural Blend of Canada and the United States

All good mechanics will be quick to give some credit for their work to the fact that they have excellent tools. In recent years we have been blessed with access to computerized data from census material and other private surveys. This technology has advanced the study of cross-cultural evangelism in an astounding way. But the scientific advancements of the '60s, 70s, and 80s have been required to keep up with the tremendous movement of people groups throughout the world.

Ray Bakke, urban specialist for the Lausanne Committee for World Evangelization, tells about the one-square-mile area of inner-city Chicago where he lives with 60,000 other people. He has discovered that there are people residing there from 60 different nations! There are only 223 in the whole world.

It is widely known that the Cubans are in Miami, the Mexicans are in Los Angeles, the Puerto Ricans are in New York, and the Polish are in Chicago. For years Blacks have heavily populated the industrialized cities in the South, and many Native Americans settled in Arizona. But the surprising truth is that ethnic change has infiltrated nearly every corner of America.

Out of the civil rights movement of the '60s has emerged a pride of color, culture, and ethnicity. People are aware of and treasure both their ethnic roots and their identity as Americans and Canadians. There is a new recognition that it is all right to be Black, Native American, Cambodian, Korean, etc., and still be a patriotic American.

It is one thing to recognize the ethnic diversity of our land and quite another to realize the direction in which this is developing. Most of us can look around and appreciate the variety of skin color that God has put within our cities. But we do not always find it easy to accept the trends that are developing. According to statistics non-Anglo people groups are likely to increase disproportionately as we roll into the 21st century. This could be because of a higher birthrate and/or immigration patterns. Look carefully at the yearly averages of immigrants who entered the United States in the decades from the '30s up to the present:

1930s	53,000 per year
1940s	104,000
1950s	252,000
1960s	332,000
1970s	429,000
1980s	570,000 (plus)

These are figures that do not include the undocumented (illegal) aliens that enter each year. The recent Immigration Act passed by Congress has done nothing to stop the daily flow of illegal aliens pouring into the United States.

The numbers also do not include the hundreds of thousands of aliens with nonimmigrant status who live legally in the United States. Falling into this category are students, temporary workers, visitors, traders, and investors, as well as their spouses and children.

This is our country. Dr. C. Peter Wagner of Fuller Seminary speaks of it as a nation of "ethnics blended into an urban stewpot." In the recent celebration of the birthday of the Statue of Liberty, the United States appeared to recommit itself to being a nation that, in the immortal words of Emma Lazarus, invites the world to "give me your tired, your poor, your huddled masses yearning to breathe free." Dr. Oscar Romo and the Southern Baptist Language Missions Department states it this way: "It is unlikely any other nation in the world is so intentionally pluralistic: the people of the United States have chosen to come to these shores: men, women and children giving up home and family, status and stability, human beings drawn by things more powerful than might or wealth; for here triumphs the concept of freedom and hope, here promises a fresh start, an equal chance: the opportunity to be somebody."[1]

So one of the benefits of reaching across cultures and forming a multicongregational church is seeing our world as it really is. It is recognizing our ethnic diversity and celebrating the rainbow mix that God has created. If the Anglo culture and the English language are requirements for acceptance into evangelical churches, we will never reach a vast majority of the people in our neighborhoods. There is compensation for those acquainting themselves with other cultures so that they can coexist in unity and serve God together.

2. THE SPIRITUAL DIVIDEND:
The Reward of Fulfilling the Great Commission
Right in Our Own Backyard

Although all four Gospels record the Great Commission, the statement made by Christ in the first chapter of the Book of Acts speaks of the power that is needed to fulfill it. As Jesus was standing with His disciples before His ascension, they asked Him a question that was puzzling them. "Lord, will you at this time restore the kingdom to Israel?" But He pushed aside this type of speculation, regarding it as irrelevant to the important issues at hand. "It is not for you to know times or seasons which the Father has fixed by his own authority. But you shall receive power when the Holy Spirit has come upon you; and you shall be my witnesses in Jerusalem and in all Judea and Samaria and to the end of the earth" (vv. 6-8).

The one thing uppermost in the mind of our blessed Lord was to instruct these future leaders on where to spread the gospel. He had a concern that the message of hope through His death and resurrection be spread to the people of all nations.

Centuries earlier it had not been God's intention for the Israelites in the Old Testament to withhold the truth about Him from their Gentile neighbors. He had begun a work in the Israelite nation that was to have spread to all nations.

But it was much later that the gospel of Jesus first took root in a small ethnic group of Galilean Jews. Jesus had no intentions of this truth remaining only within that group. He specifically commanded them to carry the message to the ethnics (nations) of the world.

God in recent years has sent Canadians and Americans as missionaries to communicate His light to many lands. They have fulfilled much of the Great Commission. For reasons known only to himself, God has now targeted us to receive an influx of people from the nations of the world. It is still essential to send missionaries overseas, but it has become imperative that trained workers be sent to reach cross-culturally the masses here at home. Their eternal destination depends on this.

There is satisfaction in being a part of a missionary society that promotes and supports a worldwide mission program. But in addition to this to be actively participating in a mission venture here at home will bring you joy and a challenge beyond description.

The spreading of the gospel is the most rewarding endeavor any follower of Christ can experience. Perhaps this is because it was born in the heart of God. Churches and pastors can discover the diversity of people groups in their neighborhood and become directly involved in the fulfillment of the Great Commission.

3. THE STRATEGIC DIVIDEND:
The Reward of Resources Effectively and Efficiently Used

The first two rewards can be achieved because of a renewed vision of ethnic America as a mission field. But there is also a reward in evangelizing this field through the resources God has put within each church.

There are four things that almost every church will have: a building, personnel, time, and finances. Though there never seems to be enough of any one of these, they are "loaves and fishes" that Christ will multiply as we dedicate them for His service. Don't forget, we have a Senior Partner. We are not in this business alone!

a. BUILDINGS. Even the most aggressive church program will probably use its buildings only a few hours each day. Even then there are some areas of the building, such as the sanctuary, that are used far less than others.

As keepers of the house of God, we are to encourage good stewardship and remind the church that God loves a "cheerful giver" (2 Cor. 9:7). As the people cheerfully release their buildings for multiple use, some interesting things will happen.

One of the blessings will be church growth. It has been pointed out that church growth is often experienced when people are given precedence over buildings, and when buildings are not so elaborate as to alienate individuals who have a meager standard of living.

Spiritual gain will be felt by a congregation that shares its facilities with other language groups for the purpose of evangelism.

The bottom line question in this business of use of and sharing of buildings is this: "Does the building really belong to a certain group of people, or does it in the highest and best sense belong to God to be used as He directs? Were not all the monies given to erect and maintain the building and property given 'as to the Lord'?"

b. PERSONNEL. Not only does God desire the salvation of all people, but also He has a plan to reach every culture on the face of this planet. It is our responsibility to find the area in which God wants us to be used to help fulfill His plan.

Everyone will not be reached with the same method. People respond individually. But it is certain that God uses people to present the gospel, and this seems to be a universal ingredient in each plan of salvation. Because of this the adequate training and commissioning of ethnic workers and cross-cultural pastors is mandatory.

There are great benefits for the leader who will sacrifice time and effort to train one person to reach a certain ethnic group in a particular neighborhood. Extensive research is needed to analyze an area and prayerfully choose the person who is best suited to pastor in that particular place. After that very important work has been finished, the newly appointed pastor must surround himself with leaders and helpers who are willing to help get the task done.

c. TIME. Time management is probably the most important factor in multiple-building use. Activities must be scheduled in a way that is fair and equitable to each congregation. It is essential that the buildings be assigned to each group when it is convenient and beneficial to the people meeting there.

For example, if there are two groups meeting on Sunday morning, which one will have their service first? Ask the congregation who traditionally has the shortest service to meet first. This will eliminate impatient parishioners from waiting for the first group to finish. It is important that a calendar for building use be posted in a prominent place.

d. FINANCE. Most local churches do not have enough income to meet the needs of buildings, salaries, and other budgetary items. To sponsor the planting of a new church, including the securing of real estate and a building, is beyond what most existing local churches can do. However, there are financial advantages to the use of an existing building as a multicongregational plant.

—There are many expenses that are not increased significantly by the adding of a new congregation. These might include building payments, insurance, most utilities, and janitorial services.

—The new congregation will not have the above expenses that would be incurred in a schoolhouse, rented building, or home. They, therefore, might be able to contribute to the building costs. There is also a possibility that the district would be able to contribute money from the Home Mission budget to help in the expenses in the beginning. Your district leader will be able to give you this information.

—The missionary society might want to get involved by helping to finance an exciting mission opportunity, a new ethnic church. This would be a revenue that would not use tithes and offerings that have been committed for other items.

—God always blesses a church that reaches out in compassion to newcomers to this nation. Our average giving increased and seems to stretch much farther to meet the needs of the local congregation.

Another dividend for the church that opens their doors for multicongregational use is the knowledge that someone will accept the Lord who otherwise might have missed the way. Successful social ministry is necessary, for we must love and care for the poor even as Jesus did. But let us find our greatest gain in the changed life, the new soul, and the lost that are found.

---

1. Quoted by C. Peter Wagner in a speech to the National Convocation on Evangelizing Ethnic America, April 15, 1985, Houston, from a brochure from the Southern Baptist Language Missions Department.

Conclusion

While immigrants arrive at jet plane speed, the Church is traveling at a sailboat's pace to meet them. It is obvious that the Church of Jesus Christ in Canada and the United States is not successfully dealing with the influx of immigrants from all over the world. Churches are not being started at the rate needed to keep up with the number of new people arriving from other countries to take up residence. Evangelism methods are woefully lacking in giving these newcomers an opportunity to choose to follow Jesus. Strategies for reaching the many Muslims, Buddhists, Shintoists, and adherents of other religions flooding our country are nearly nonexistent.

Combined with this inertia is a basic prejudice that exists in every community. Our various racial and cultural heritages strongly influence how we treat each other. More often than not, the treatment we give one another is detrimental to the unity of our country. Racial and cultural prejudice does not automatically go away when we get close to one another; on the contrary, it usually increases. The irony is that the closer we live to each other physically, the farther we become emotionally, spiritually, and socially, because of the protective and prejudicial barriers we erect.

As previously stated, this secular cultural concept has been allowed to creep into our churches. We cannot accomplish the Great Commission with such attitudes of prejudice and separation.

How then should believers act in the midst of this crisis? What principles should govern our behavior toward others who are not of our racial and/or cultural background? There are some lessons that Jesus teaches us in His handling of the cross-cultural confrontation with the Samaritan woman at the well.

To understand this incident, we need to review ancient

history. In 722 B.C. the Jews were taken into captivity by the Assyrians. This was the final fall of the Northern Kingdom of Israel. Part of the Jews were deported to Assyria to live. Captives from surrounding nations were moved into the Northern Kingdom. This was an effort to weaken the Jews and prevent them from revolting. The Jews that remained in the Northern Kingdom lived side by side with their new neighbors. Eventually many of them intermarried, thus destroying the ethnic purity of which the Jews were so proud. These cross-cultural marriages caused those of the Southern Jews to regard their Northern neighbors as half-breeds. They would not allow them to participate in any of their activities, especially religious celebrations. When Jesus came to the well and encountered the Samaritan women, the feelings were still very strong.

An interesting phrase is recorded in John 4. In his account of Jesus and the disciples' trip to Galilee, John wrote, "He [Jesus] had to pass through Samaria." Even though Samaria was directly between Judea and Galilee, most Jews "had" to travel around Samaria. When we consider the history of hatred between the Jews and Samaritans, it is amazing to think that Jesus had to travel through Samaria.

Why would Jesus make such a decision? Doubtless it was because He knew that a woman and a group of her relatives and friends were in need and would be responsive to the presentation He was prepared to make.

So Jesus teaches us the first lesson on how we should act in the midst of this cultural crisis in the Church in Canada and the United States.

LESSON NUMBER ONE:

Spiritual Needs in People's Lives Must Take Precedence over Any Cultural Differences.

Cultural norms, standards, and preferences that seem valuable are not nearly as important as people and their spiritual needs. This must be true, not only as we attempt to evangelize cross-culturally, but also in every area of our personal lives. We cannot let the world and its preconceived ideas dictate to us who and what we should be and with whom we should associate.

Jesus' route through Samaria was not only the shortest route but also a route toward a definite need that He knew existed there. Jesus was willing to take the first step to establish common relationships with the Samaritan woman. Although there was immense hatred between the Jews and the Samaritans, there was a common love for Jacob. So, rather than dwelling on their differences, Jesus started by meeting her at Jacob's well—a patriarch accepted by both cultures.

Jesus also asked her for a drink from the water of the well. How wise He was to recognize that many friends are made over food and drink.

In trying to find common ground between cultures, we must try to discover what makes other people tick. The communication point may be as simple as a meal, a football game, or a child. What activities and interests might be shared by you and those of other cultures? These can open doors to friendship and understanding beyond your expectations.

Jesus taught us that cultural differences must be subservient to spiritual needs. But there are more lessons to be learned from the Master.

LESSON NUMBER TWO:

Spiritual Truth from the Scripture Is More Important than Any Cultural Differences.

Jesus in His conversation with the Samaritan woman soon got to the point. He began to talk to her about her past husbands and present lover. He was getting personal; doubtless she didn't like it very much. But remember that Jesus had arrived at this point in the conversation because He was will-

117

ing to talk to her as a woman (forbidden in Jewish culture) and because He was willing to drink from her water bucket (also forbidden in His culture). Common ground had been established. Jesus had earned the right to talk to her about more personal things because He had been willing to put aside prejudicial cultural differences and speak to her on an equal basis.

To get away from a subject she did not want to be on, the woman quickly turned to the matter of where one should go to church. She tried to put Jesus on the defensive, referring to Him and His people as "you," that is, the Jews.

Her arguments on this subject were the same as those of her ancestors. In other words, she was presenting a historical argument based on what she had been taught by her culture down through the years.

It should be noted that the woman had referred to cultural issues earlier in the conversation, but Jesus had ignored them. Now, however, she names God and makes Him a cultural issue. On this subject, Jesus could not be silent. He quickly (vv. 21-22) points out that what she had been taught by her ancestors was out of line with the truth. He knew the Word of God and spoke with authority.

In doing this, Jesus taught us a key lesson. When a cultural practice or belief comes in direct conflict with the Word of God, that practice or belief is wrong and must be rejected. Another way of saying this is that the test of whether a point in one's culture is to be accepted or rejected is to find out if it is or is not in conflict with God's written Word, the Bible.

Jesus' answer to the Samaritan woman was basically this: "The time has come when God is not interested in how we worship, but that we worship with a correct heart, based on spirit and truth." And that is the basic task of the Church today. We must bring people together from all cultures to worship with a right heart and to worship the one true God in spirit and in truth.

What we desperately need in this day is Christians who will commit themselves to worship together, without surrendering their cultural distinctions, but rather submitting them all to the authority of the Word of God. These bands of Christians should be representative of the cultural diversity of their communities and thus a testimony to the difference that God's Spirit makes in our lives. They must decide to let Christianity be descriptive of who they are, people united under the banner of holiness unto the Lord. With Scripture as their Guide, they will be willing to put aside differences of color and culture and open the doors of the church to all who live in a community. By this method small bands of multicongregations can spread across our land and become a vivid testimony to God's love for all mankind.

Obviously, Christianity does not stop people from being Black, White, Hispanic, Oriental, or of any other ethnic description. But through Christian worship centers of multicongregations we can break down fences and expand our horizons.

The cultural implications of this scriptural lesson are clear. Tension and division caused by cultural differences cannot be tolerated in the Church. In fact, we must find ways to break these barriers. So often these tensions and divisions are fueled by selfishness because we wish to protect what we feel are our rights and keep ourselves from having to face the unfamiliar. But God in His Word has clearly taught us that the unity and fellowship of all believers is to have priority over our prejudice and cultural differences.

Especially of note is the fact that Jesus did not let His disciples (returning from getting food for Him) stop Him from doing what He knew was right. He simply set out to instruct them about the harvest and the importance of reaping it even when it was among people with whom they were not familiar.

When Jesus spoke to His disciples about the harvest of

the ripe fields, it was as though He opened their eyes to the spiritual harvest all around them. As He stretched His arms to illustrate, no doubt the eyes of the disciples were turned to the crowd advancing toward them from the Samaritan woman's village of Sychar. Jesus had taught them, and now they had an immediate chance to put it into practice. And for several days they labored there, reaping the harvest of souls.

All pastors who find themselves in multicultural neighborhoods must open their own eyes and realize what God is calling them to do. We must not run! We can start today to improve our situation and begin to win all ethnic people in our area, including our own culture. Just remember these lessons:

—First begin educating your people to understand God's principles on unity. Show them lovingly that His plan is to reach all peoples without being separated by culture or race. Help them see the mission field at your doorstep and let them feel your heart as you share the joy in fulfilling the Great Commission.

—Then begin slowly to start some cross-cultural outreach. Involve your people and let them see what a thrill it is to learn other people's ways.

—Watch carefully for an opportunity to develop these new outreaches into fellowships and then worship centers. Begin to train and establish leadership and nurture this "new baby." Who knows, you may even see it come into full adulthood.

—Give attention to an overall organization that will allow your congregation to coexist with the new congregation with the least amount of tension.

God has placed this opportunity before you. As a body of believers you must not allow culture to stand in the way of God's plan of evangelizing your neighborhood. If you and I make the commitment to reach those around us, many will come to know Christ because they will have seen Him in action within our lives. And others will follow our example, thus making a greater impact on the mission field that is all around us.

APPENDIX

✱ QUESTIONNAIRE ✱

Multicongregational Committee

LOS ANGELES DISTRICT

PURPOSE

The convening of this committee was initiated by Dr. Paul Benefiel for the purpose of delineating parameters within which both existing and future multicongregational churches could function and flourish. In order to help in making these decisions, it was decided by the committee to create and administer a nationwide survey of churches already multicongregational to discover any patterns that would help us in our deliberations. A copy of the instrument is at the end of this report.

GENESIS OF THE QUESTIONNAIRE

The responsibility of creating the questionnaire was given to two people, Glen Van Dyne and Tim Kauffman,* who formulated and presented a final copy for revisions to the committee. The committee members gave some suggestions to the authors, most of which were incorporated into the final product.

All of the multicongregations on the Los Angeles District, and as many other multicongregational Nazarene churches as we could find from other sources, were sent the questionnaire. In all, 102 questionnaires were sent, and 50 were filled out and returned: 20 from the Los Angeles District, 29 from the rest of the United States, and 1 from Canada. In the 20 L.A. responses, 30 ethnic/language (E/L) congregations were represented, and in the 30 responses from the rest of the continent, 47 congregations were described, making a total of 77 congregations in all.

_____

*J. Timothy Kauffman, graduate of Eastern Nazarene College and Nazarene Theological Seminary; currently Ph.D. candidate at Fuller Theological Seminary. He is also presently executive director of W.O.U.R.L.D. PROJECT.

LIMITATIONS

The questionnaire itself does have limitations. Because the instrument is closed-ended, the relatively few answers may not have given enough choices for highly individualized situations. Any future questionnaire should include at least several additional choices.

A second possible negative point is that the questions about (1) the financial arrangements (No. 5), (2) how the E/L groups were chosen (No. 7), (3) the past problems (No. 9), and (4) the current problems (No. 10) in this ministry very often had multiple answers. The obstacles this brings are, first, that it is more difficult to pinpoint the one or two significant issues. Second, the waters become even more muddy when there are three to nine congregations within a given multicongregational structure all having the same answers. The question to ask is, are these truly problems for each of these congregations (which is possible), or did the pastor lump them all together for convenience?

The upside to this question is that we can get a hierarchy of problems and some intimations of where these churches are going. The future questionnaires should probably ask for 1, 2, 3 priority answers for those kinds of questions.

A third limitation, and almost certainly an increasing issue with incredible ramifications, was that a good number of the pastors questioned had inherited the multicongregational church; and some, through their answers and comments, expressed feelings ranging from frustration and bare toleration to washing of their hands of the issue.

Nevertheless, it should be possible to come up with significant data from this questionnaire. Where there may be a question about complete scientific validity, we still will have uncovered areas that give reason for joy, concern, debate, or food for future inquiry.

DELIMITATIONS

In order not to complicate relationships, the fragility of which we were unsure, we decided to send this questionnaire only to the senior pastors of the sponsoring churches. We realize that the full picture can only be painted when all the pastors have been surveyed. Each pastor to whom the questionnaire was sent was encouraged to go through the questionnaire with the E/L pastors.

A further decision was made to include the black churches into the sponsoring churches and not into the E/L category. The reasons for this are (1) that those churches are historically American and speak English, and (2) that all are, in fact, churches sponsoring E/L congregations.

TERMINOLOGY

Because of the both trite and prejudicial character of the word *ethnic,* we felt it necessary to look for a term that would be clear and not misleading, yet not prejudicial. We did not find that word. So we chose a combination term, *ethnic/language* (E/L), in order to include the perception that most E/L congregations, in southern California at least, are formed because of language barriers rather than ethnicity.

GENERAL SURVEY RESULTS

The following material is a general summary of the data based only on two categories, those being according to Los Angeles and those of the U.S. For the purpose of keeping these two separate, we have given those E/L churches on the L.A. District the designation "L.A." and the E/L congregations in the rest of the country and Canada, "OTHER." When we combine them and take all the data together, we call this "COMBINED."

Whenever there is a slash, the number on the left is the raw data, and the number on the right is the percentage of those E/L congregations who crossed that answer on the questionnaire. Some marked more than one answer, making the percentages add up to more than 100%.

A careful examination of these numbers alone will help the reader understand how L.A. approaches the E/L congregation differently from its U.S. counterparts. In addition, issues will begin to take shape, and problem areas will commence to crystallize.

1. Which of these descriptions best explains how your multicongregational church is organized?

COMBINED	OTHER	L.A.	
12/16%*	3/ 6%**	9/30%**	a. One church with more than one senior pastor.
26/34%	22/47%	4/13%	b. One senior pastor with ethnic pastors functioning as assistant pastors.

127

COMBINED	OTHER	L.A.	
29/38%	15/32%	14/47%	c. More than one church each with a senior pastor.
2/ 1%	1/ 0%	1/ 3%	d. I'm unsure just how we function together.
9/12%	7/15%	2/ 7%	e. One pastor over all of the congregation.
0/ 0%	0/ 0%	0/ 0%	f. Other.

2. Where did you find the pastoral leadership for your ethnic/language (E/L) congregation(s)?

COMBINED	OTHER	L.A.	
21/27%	15/32%	6/20%	a. He approached me about the possibility.
27/35%	8/17%	19/63%	b. Through the district leadership.
2/ 3%	2/ 4%	0/ 0%	c. From one of our Nazarene educational facilities.
17/22%	14/30%	3/10%	d. Through denominational contacts.
14/18%	13/28%	1/ 3%	e. As a result of a personal search.
2/ 3%	1/ 2%	1/ 3%	f. Someone in our church knew someone.
15/ 9%	11/23%	4/13%	g. Other.

3. What are the names of the ethnic/language Nazarene congregations presently meeting in your church facility?

No. Ethnic/language group					How long in existence?		Avg. attendance in main service?		
COMBINED	OTHER	L.A.			L.A.	OTHER	L.A.	OTHER	TOTAL ATT.
1/ 1%	1/ 2%	0/ 0%	r.	West Indian	---	27.0	--	180	180
3/ 4%	2/ 4%	1/ 3%	c.	Native American	0.5	---	--	108	108
4/ 5%	0/ 0%	4/13%	e.	Armenian	4.8	---	94	--	94
3/ 4%	3/ 6%	0/ 0%	j.	Haitian	---	2.0	--	92	92
1/ 1%	1/ 2%	0/ 0%	l.	Kanjobal-Ind. Guat.	---	0.5	--	90	90
4/ 5%	4/ 9%	0/ 0%	d.	Cambodian	---	5.6	--	73	73
1/ 1%	1/ 2%	0/ 0%	q.	Samoan	---	---	--	60	60
31/40%	15/32%	16/53%	a.	Spanish speaking	5.3	3.1	43	55	49
10/13%	6/13%	4/13%	b.	Korean	3.0	3.0	61	25	41
1/ 1%	1/ 2%	0/ 0%	m.	Finnish	---	2.0	--	40	40
3/ 4%	1/ 2%	2/ 7%	f.	Arabic speaking	3.0	2.0	43	25	37
4/ 5%	3/ 6%	1/ 3%	i.	Filipino	4.0	---	45	28	33
1/ 1%	0/ 0%	1/ 3%	g.	Chinese (Formosan)	4.0	---	30	--	30

COMBINED	OTHER	L.A.			L.A.	OTHER	L.A.	OTHER	ATT.
3/ 4%	3/ 6%	0/ 0%	k.	Laotian	---	3.3	--	26	26
1/ 1%	1/ 2%	0/ 0%	o.	Vietnamese	---	2.0	--	25	25
4/ 5%	3/ 6%	1/ 3%	h.	Chinese (Mandarin)	1.0	6.3	27	9	23
1/ 1%	1/ 2%	0/ 0%	p.	German	---	4.0	--	18	18
1/ 1%	1/ 2%	0/ 0%	n.	Jamaican	---	0.2	--	15	15

4. How would you describe your congregation right now? If you have more than one E/L group, instead of checking, please write the letter of the appropriate group you marked in your answer to question No. 3 in the blank.

COMBINED	OTHER	L.A.	
10/13%	4/ 8%	6/20%	a. Bible study.
21/27%	17/36%	4/13%	b. Small congregation(s) administered by the board of the sponsoring congregation.
0/ 0%	0/ 0%	0/ 0%	c. Large congregation(s) administered by the board of the sponsoring congregation.
16/34%	8/17%	8/27%	d. Small congregation(s) unorganized but with its own governing body.
7/ 9%	4/ 8%	3/10%	e. Large congregation(s) organized separately.
21/27%	11/23%	10/33%	f. Small congregation(s) organized separately.
1/ 1%	1/ 1%	0/ 0%	g. Organized together.

5. What are the financial arrangements agreed to with the other congregation(s)?

COMBINED	OTHER	L.A.	
28/36%	23/49%	5/17%	a. The sponsoring church has asked nothing of the E/L congregation because they are too small to be asked.
12/16%	8/17%	4/13%	b. The sponsoring congregation is subsidizing the E/L congregation.
20/26%	14/30%	6/20%	c. The E/L congregation pays rent to the sponsoring congregation.
18/23%	5/11%	13/43%	d. The E/L congregation contributes a percentage of its income to help pay for building use. What percentage? _____
3/ 4%	0/ 0%	3/10%	e. The E/L congregation contributes its full proportional share to the cost of operating the building facilities.
3/ 4%	1/ 2%	2/ 7%	f. Other.

6. Is there a <u>written</u> agreement between all the congregations meeting in the building concerning, for example, the use and allocation of space, finances, equipment, etc.?

L.A.		OTHER	
Yes	No	Yes	No
9/30%	20/70%	8/17%	39/83%

7. On what basis did you choose the E/L group(s) you have targeted?

ALL	OTHER	L.A.	
14/18%	5/11%	9/30%	a. A demographic survey from personal research or other research group. If other group, which? _____
27/35%	18/38%	9/30%	b. There were several families of this/these E/L group(s) interested in services.
23/30%	16/34%	7/23%	c. It was impossible to overlook all the people of this/these E/L group(s) on the streets of our city.
21/27%	14/30%	7/23%	d. God laid these people on our heart.
9/12%	2/ 4%	7/23%	e. We had a leader from this group volunteer to lead them.
2/ 3%	2/ 4%	0/ 0%	f. A non-Nazarene church approached us about using our building.
9/12%	3/ 6%	6/20%	g. Other

8. Do the congregations, meeting in your building, plan for:

   a. Regular combined services?

L.A.		OTHER	
Yes	No	Yes	No
16/53%	9/30%	20/43%	26/55%

   b. Times of fellowship?

L.A.		OTHER	
Yes	No	Yes	No
22/73%	6/20%	35/74%	10/21%

9. What problems have you had in the past in this kind of ministry, and what did you do to solve them? (Check all that are appropriate.)

COMBINED	OTHER	L.A.	
37/48%	23/49%	14/47%	a. Financial.
7/ 9%	2/ 4%	5/17%	b. In my relationships with the other pastor.
21/27%	10/21%	11/37%	c. In the relationships between congregations.
16/21%	12/26%	4/13%	d. Lack of written material on the subject.
17/22%	6/13%	11/37%	e. Scheduling.

COMBINED	OTHER	L.A.	
16/21%	9/19%	7/23%	f. Inability to develop the leadership potential in the E/L pastor(s).
15/19%	7/15%	8/27%	g. Personal lack of education in leading multi-cultural congregations.
13/17%	10/21%	3/10%	h. Other. (Nine of 10 were one HCC.)

10. Do you have problems today with which you would appreciate help in resolving?

COMBINED	OTHER	L.A.	
6/ 8%	4/ 9%	2/ 7%	a. You need a model to follow.
16/21%	12/25%	4/13%	b. You would like more resource material.
17/22%	7/15%	10/33%	c. You would have appreciated courses in how to begin and organize a multicongregational structure.
12/16%	5/11%	7/23%	d. You feel the need for informed supervision.
9/12%	9/19%	0/ 0%	e. You find yourself hoping for a course you could take in how to manage a multicongregational church.
16/21%	7/15%	9/30%	f. You find that no one seems to understand the issues at stake in this new area of ministry.
40/52%	23/49%	17/57%	g. You would take advantage of any responsible information or practical help in the area of urban ministry that was offered you.
9/12%	4/ 9%	5/17%	h. Other.

14. Would you be willing to take part in an information network that will attempt to provide support and understanding of how our church can be even more effective in reaching the many cultural groups in our country?

	Yes	N/A	No
COMBINED	67/87%	6/ 8%	4/ 5%

15. Would you appreciate our sending you a copy of our report?

	Yes	N/A	No
COMBINED	71/92%	3/ 4%	3/ 4%

*Overall percentage of answers given to this question.
**Percentages of answers given in L.A. and OTHER to this question.

FURTHER ANALYSIS OF THE QUESTIONNAIRE

As we begin to look at this material one question at a time, we will begin to see significant parallels, and at times we will sort the

131

data base differently to give us a more exact look at the issues and dynamics at work in the congregations we are examining. Because the nature of this questionnaire was to give to the committee a greater understanding of these issues and dynamics, most of what we will be doing is to ask questions and try to see short-range and long-range significance. We do not claim that this instrument is a precise scientific tool.

Analysis of Question No. I:

The largest discrepancy in the answers given to this question is found in the answers to *a* and *b*. The perception of the church being unified, yet with an E/L structure, and each E/L congregation having its own senior pastor, seems to be a typically L.A. District concept. There are at least two main reasons for this: (1) We have several knowledgeable pastors who are committed to this philosophy, and their ideas have influenced others; and (2) several pastors have attended classes at Fuller School of World Mission and have hammered out their ideas on the anvil of the issues presented there.

The rest of this country prefers to have E/L pastors functioning as assistants. This could cause the E/L pastors and their congregations to feel like second-class citizens. But there might be an advantage while the E/L congregation is small to having a staff relationship.

As with all of these categories, when sorted accordingly, this one yields much data that would take much more time to sift through than we have at our disposal. However, there are several things that stand out. First, 36% of those churches that have one church with more than one senior pastor *(a)* have a written agreement with their E/L congregations. On the other hand, only 8% of those with ethnic pastors functioning as assistants *(b)* have such.

Second, those answering with *a* have a 90% rate for having combined services, whereas *b* and *c* have 40%-45% success. In addition to these, we have sorted the data on the basis of how the church is organized. We then determined what and how many problems were named and what help was needed for each category. We gave, for example, the problem that was named the most often under the rubric of "1*a* Org." the number 1, the second number 2, etc. The object was to see which problems or help was most prevalent when certain organizational styles were made. Of course, this is not absolute, but there is quite a bit of difference.

How the Church Is Organized Versus the Problems of the Past and Present Help Needed

1. HOW IS THE CHURCH ORGANIZED?	Problems (9) a	b	c	d	e	f	g	h		1. HOW ORGANIZED	Help Needed (10) a	b	c	d	e	f	g	h
a. One church—more than one pastor	3	7	1	7	2	4	7			a.	7	3	1	5	3	1	5	
b. One senior pastor—ethnic assistants	1	6	6	4	5	3	2			b.	4	2	3	3	7	5	1	5
c. More than one church—each senior	1	7	2	2	4	6	5			c.	7	3	4	5	6	2	1	
d. This answer was given only once																		
e. Other	2	3	1	6	5	3	6			e.	2	4	4	4	3	4	1	

Fig. 1

Each of the church organization structures carries with it certain kinds of problems. For example, the No. 1 problem of 1*a* is not the No. 1 problem of 1*b*. In order to figure out which problems needed help, check the questionnaire, questions Nos. 9 and 10.

Analysis of Question No. 2:

This question was geared to determine just how the E/L congregations found their leadership. Over 63% of the congregations in L.A. found their pastors through district leadership. There are several possible explanations for this, all of which intertwine. It could be due to the Thrust to the Cities, with the district involvement and the goals of the program to plant churches. Also, there is a deep commitment within district leadership to establish E/L congregations.

However, the issue has larger ramifications. When district leadership plays an active role in the establishment of E/L congregations, if not directly then through guidelines, we see that the likelihood of an all-important written agreement rises significantly, the finances take on a completely different hue, and combined church services also are more likely to occur (see Fig. 2).

The finance figures point up some possible dangers. It is probably best to formulate them as questions. In subsidizing our E/L congregations here, are we subconsciously treating them here as we might on the mission field? Even if that is not our intention, is that the way they perceive us? If so, how does that make them feel about

133

giving and our feelings about them? It is borne out by the survey that as soon as the E/L pastors and congregations are treated as equals spiritually, emotionally, and financially, they will return the respect placed in them.

Using District Leadership's Effect on Finances, Services, and Contracts

	Contract Yes	Services Yes
Approached by someone	20%	44%
District leadership	35%	71%
Denominational contacts	0%	100%
Personal search	6%	31%

Finances:
Out of 30 E/L churches in L.A., 16 (53%) contribute something or all.
Out of 47 E/L churches in OTHER, 5 (11%) contribute something or all.

Fig. 2

Analysis of Question No. 6:

This brings us to the importance of a contract or some written agreement. Several pastors wrote in their questionnaires that they had inherited the E/L situation, and most were open about either not wanting to deal with it or being frustrated and helpless in the face of "someone else's doing." None of these men had contracts with which to operate.

This issue is going to be an increasing problem if it is not dealt with decisively. Pastors with enough vision to begin an E/L congregation should also be able to see the ramifications of not having something to which a future pastor can refer.

Let's look at the effects of sorting the data on the basis of having or not having a contract and see its effect on having combined services and fellowship together.

What do these figures show us? Is it that where there is a contract, there is greater commitment? Or does it have something to do with seeing the E/L congregation as an equal partner within the Christian worshiping community, which, when treated as such, will respond in kind?

Those who reported no contract also had a completely different set of problems, both past and present. A look at these in Figure 4 will help us to draw some conclusions. We used the same rating system as in Figure 1.

134

Contract Versus Services and Fellowship

	Yes, Have Service Without Sort		
		L.A.	OTHER
Those Having Combined Services: Without Contract:	35%	53%	43%
With Contract:	66%		
Those Having Regular Fellowship: Without Contract:	68%	74%	74%
With Contract:	94%		

Fig. 3

It is difficult to know just how to interpret some of the interesting observations in this figure. It is easy to understand a pastor's concern about developing leaders and being troubled about a personal lack of education in this field, but why is it that pastors who say they have contracts also have more difficulty with congregational relations and scheduling than those who have no agreement?

Problems Past

Contract:

No	Yes	Issue
1	2	Finances
7	5	Relations with the other E/L pastors
6	1	Relations with the E/L congregations
4	4	Lack of written material on subject
5	3	Scheduling
2	7	Inability to develop leaders
3	6	Personal lack of education in leading E/L congregations

Problems Present

Contract:

No	Yes	Issue
5	-	You need a model to follow.
2	-	You would like more resource material.
4	3	Would have liked a course in how to begin E/L congregation.
3	-	You feel the need for informed supervision.
6	4	You wish there were a course on this subject.
7	1	No one seems to understand the issues in this new ministry.
1	2	You would welcome information or practical help.

Fig. 4

Those who have agreements with their E/L congregations see their most pressing present problems as the need for additional help and education, and feeling alone with their burden.

135

Analysis of Question No. 3:

There are several things about the size or growth patterns of the E/L groups we want to notice. The first is to see which groups are presently growing most rapidly. To ask the question "why" would make a further study necessary. Suffice it to say that it is a good exercise to see where certain E/L groups fit in the average size. For example, in our district, the Armenian congregations are doing very well. One could also ask questions about whether some groups would have growth potential, and whether other groups need more time and research.

3. What are the names of the ethnic/language Nazarene congregations presently meeting in your church facility?

| No. | | | | Ethnic/language group | How long in existence? | | Avg. attendance in main service? | | |
COMBINED	OTHER	L.A.			L.A.	OTHER	L.A.	OTHER	TOTAL ATT.
1/ 1%	1/ 2%	0/ 0%	r.	West Indian	---	27.0	--	180	180
3/ 4%	2/ 4%	1/ 3%	c.	Native American	0.5	---	--	108	108
4/ 5%	0/ 0%	4/13%	e.	Armenian	4.8	---	94	--	94
3/ 4%	3/ 6%	0/ 0%	j.	Haitian	---	2.0	--	92	92
1/ 1%	1/ 2%	0/ 0%	l.	Kanjobal-Ind. Guat.	---	0.5	--	90	90
4/ 5%	4/ 9%	0/ 0%	d.	Cambodian	---	5.6	--	73	73
1/ 1%	1/ 2%	0/ 0%	q.	Samoan	---	---	--	60	60
31/40%	15/32%	16/53%	a.	Spanish speaking	5.3	3.1	43	55	49
10/13%	6/13%	4/13%	b.	Korean	3.0	3.0	61	25	41
1/ 1%	1/ 2%	0/ 0%	m.	Finnish	---	2.0	--	40	40
3/ 4%	1/ 2%	2/ 7%	f.	Arabic speaking	3.0	2.0	43	25	37
4/ 5%	3/ 6%	1/ 3%	i.	Filipino	4.0	---	45	28	33
1/ 1%	0/ 0%	1/ 3%	g.	Chinese (Formosan)	4.0	---	30	--	30
3/ 4%	3/ 6%	0/ 0%	k.	Laotian	---	3.3	--	26	26
1/ 1%	1/ 2%	0/ 0%	o.	Vietnamese	---	2.0	--	25	25
4/ 5%	3/ 6%	1/ 3%	h.	Chinese (Mandarin)	1.0	6.3	27	9	23
1/ 1%	1/ 2%	0/ 0%	p.	German	---	4.0	--	18	18
1/ 1%	1/ 2%	0/ 0%	n.	Jamaican	---	0.2	--	15	15

Fig. 5

136

Analysis of Question No. 4:

This question was intended to find out how the E/L congregations were affiliated with the sponsoring congregation. It fulfilled its purpose. However, it may be interesting to see how each of these affiliations impacted the perception of their need for help. We must always keep in mind that the senior pastor of the sponsoring congregation is the one through whose eyes these questions were being answered.

Church Size and Organization Versus Problems and Help Needed

4 E/L Desg.	Help Needed Now a	b	c	d	e	f	g	h		Past Problems a	b	c	d	e	f	g	h
a.	6	6	2	2	6	4	1	-	A Bible study	2	-	5	5	2	2	1	3
b.	6	2	2	4	6	4	1	-	Small church administered by sponsor	1	6	4	4	4	4	3	2
c.	Only one answer								Large church administered by sponsor								
d.	6	2	3	3	6	5	1	-	Small church governing itself	2	6	2	7	1	4	5	-
e.	4	4	-	-	2	2	1	-	Large church organized separately	4	4	1	1	4	4	6	3
f.	7	3	2	6	5	3	2	-	Small church organized separately	1	7	2	3	4	5	5	-
g.	Only one answer								Organized together								

Fig. 6

Analysis of Question No. 7:

How an E/L congregation is targeted is also important. The closed-ended answers to this question could be better phrased as not to have two answers basically the same. For example, "It was impossible to overlook all the people" and "God laid these people on our heart" are two answers that have basically the same meaning. Los Angeles was definitely more research oriented, and the rest of the country more serendipitous, answering questions *b, c,* and *d.*

CONCLUSION

We are well aware that the wealth of material received from these churches has not yet been fully exploited. There will be further refinement and study of the material. Therefore, your comments, improvements, and criticisms are welcome.

There does seem to be great interest among the churches participating. First, an almost 50% return on the questionnaires is very good. Second, 92% want a copy of our report, and 87% of the informants would like to be included in an information network.

137

✳ QUESTIONNAIRE ✳

Name of Church: _____

Church Address: _____

Name of Pastor: _____

Tel. No.:   (   ) _____

1. **Which of these descriptions best explains how your multicongregational church is organized?**
   - ____ *a.* One church with more than one senior pastor.
   - ____ *b.* One senior pastor with ethnic pastors functioning as assistant pastors.
   - ____ *c.* More than one church each with a senior pastor.
   - ____ *d.* I'm unsure just how we function together.
   - ____ *e.* Other _____

2. **Where did you find the pastoral leadership for your ethnic/language (E/L) congregation(s)?**
   - ____ *a.* He approached me about the possibility.
   - ____ *b.* Through the district leadership.
   - ____ *c.* From one of our Nazarene educational facilities.
   - ____ *d.* Through denominational contacts.
   - ____ *e.* As a result of a personal search.
   - ____ *f.* Someone in our church knew someone.
   - ____ *g.* Other _____

3. **What are the names of the ethnic/language Nazarene congregations presently meeting in your church facility?**

No.	Ethnic/language group	How long in existence?	Avg. attendance in main service?
____ *a.*	Spanish speaking	____ Years	_____
____ *b.*	Korean	____ Years	_____
____ *c.*	Native American	____ Years	_____
____ *d.*	Cambodian	____ Years	_____
____ *e.*	Armenian	____ Years	_____
____ *f.*	Arabic speaking	____ Years	_____
____ *g.*	Chinese (Formosan)	____ Years	_____

No.	Ethnic/language group	How long in existence?	Avg. attendance in main service?
____ h.	Chinese (Mandarin)	____ Years	_____
____ i.	Filipino	____ Years	_____
____ j.	Other _____	____ Years	_____
____ k.	Other _____	____ Years	_____

4. **How would you describe your congregation right now? If you have more than one E/L group, instead of checking, please write the letter of the appropriate group you marked in your answer to question No. 3 in the blank.**

   ____ a. Bible study.

   ____ b. Small congregation(s) administered by the board of the sponsoring congregation.

   ____ c. Large congregation(s) administered by the board of the sponsoring congregation.

   ____ d. Small congregation(s) unorganized but with its own governing body.

   ____ e. Large congregation(s) organized separately.

   ____ f. Small congregation(s) organized separately.

   ____ g. Other _____

5. **What are the financial arrangements agreed to with the other congregation(s)?**

   ____ a. The sponsoring church has asked nothing of the E/L congregation because they are too small to be asked.

   ____ b. The sponsoring congregation is subsidizing the E/L congregation.

   ____ c. The E/L congregation pays rent to the sponsoring congregation.

   ____ d. The E/L congregation contributes a percentage of its income to help pay for building use. What percentage? _____

   ____ e. The E/L congregation contributes its full proportional share to the cost of operating the building facilities.

   ____ f. Other _____

6. **Is there a <u>written</u> agreement between all the congregations meeting in the building concerning, for example, the use and allocation of space, finances, equipment, etc.?** Yes ____ No ____

7. **On what basis did you choose the E/L group(s) you have targeted?**

_____ a. A demographic survey from personal research or other research group. If other group, which? _____

_____ b. There were several families of this/these E/L group(s) interested in services.

_____ c. It was impossible to overlook all the people of this/these E/L group(s) on the streets of our city.

_____ d. God laid these people on our heart.

_____ e. We had a leader from this group volunteer to lead them.

_____ f. A non-Nazarene church approached us about using our building.

_____ g. Other _____

8. **Do the congregations, meeting in your building, plan for:**

a. **Regular combined services?** Yes _____ No _____ How often _____

b. **Times of fellowship?** Yes _____ No _____ How often _____

9. **What problems have you had in the past in this kind of ministry, and what did you do to solve them?** (Check all that are appropriate.)

_____ a. Financial.

_____ b. In my relationships with the other pastor.

_____ c. In the relationships between congregations.

_____ d. Lack of written material on the subject.

_____ e. Scheduling.

_____ f. Inability to develop the leadership potential in the E/L pastor(s).

_____ g. Personal lack of education in leading multicultural congregations.

_____ h. Other _____

Please explain how you solved this/these problem(s):

With sponsoring congregation	With E/L congregation
_____	_____
_____	_____
_____	_____
_____	_____

10. **Do you have problems today with which you would appreciate help in resolving?**
    ____ a. You need a model to follow.
    ____ b. You would like more resource material.
    ____ c. You would have appreciated courses in how to begin and organize a multicongregational structure.
    ____ d. You feel the need for informed supervision.
    ____ e. You find yourself hoping for a course you could take in how to manage a multicongregational church.
    ____ f. You find that no one seems to understand the issues at stake in this new area of ministry.
    ____ g. You would take advantage of any responsible information or practical help in the area of urban ministry that was offered you.
    ____ h. Other _____

    If you need to explain further, you may refer to the lettered problems and describe briefly below.

    _____
    _____
    _____
    _____

11. **Do you know of any other church(es), of another denomination in your area, who are having success with a multicongregational ministry? If so, who?**
    Name: Address: Tel. No.:

    _____
    _____
    _____
    _____

12. **Have you found any resources or help from other groups of assistance to your effort? If so, which?**
    Name: Address: Tel. No.:

    _____
    _____
    _____
    _____

13. Would you please send us copies of any written documents, guide-lines, or organizational charts you may have that are related to your multicultural ministry? These will help us greatly.

14. Would you be willing to take part in an information network that will attempt to provide support and understanding of how our church can be even more effective in reaching the many cultural groups in our country? Yes _____ No _____

15. Would you appreciate our sending you a copy of our report? Yes _____ No _____

Multicongregational Committee
Los Angeles District
Church of the Nazarene
1546 E. Washington Blvd.
Pasadena, CA 91104

Bibliography

APPLEBY, JERRY L. *Missions Have Come Home to America: The Church's Cross-cultural Ministry to Ethnics.* Kansas City: Beacon Hill Press of Kansas City, 1986.

BALDA, WESLEY D. *Heirs of the Same Promise.* Arcadia, Calif.: National Convocation on Evangelizing Ethnic America, 1984.

BOLLES, RICHARD NELSON. *What Color Is Your Parachute?* Berkeley, Calif.: Ten Speed Press, 1988.

BRISCOE, D. STUART. *Genesis.* Vol. 1 of *The Communicator's Commentary.* Lloyd J. Ogilvie, ed. 21 vols. Waco, Tex.: Word Books, Publisher, 1983.

DAYTON, EDWARD R. *That Everyone May Hear.* Monrovia, Calif.: Missions Advanced Research and Communication Center, 1983.

GREENLEAF, ROBERT K. *Servant Leadership.* New York: Paulist Press, 1977.

HURN, RAYMOND W. *Mission Action Sourcebook.* Kansas City: Beacon Hill Press of Kansas City, 1982.

IMAI, MASAAKI. *Never Take Yes for an Answer.* Tokyo: Simul Press, 1975.

Japan: Its Land, People, and Culture. Tokyo: Japanese National Commission for UNESCO, 1958.

JONES, EZRA EARL, and WILSON, ROBERT. *What's Ahead for Old First Church.* New York: Harper and Row, 1974.

KLUCKHOHN, CLYDE, and MURRAY, HENRY. *Personality in Nature, Society, and Culture.* New York: Alfred A. Knopf, 1948.

LEWIN, KERT. "Frontiers in Group Dynamics." *Human Relations* 1 (1947): 13-40.

MURDOCK, GEORGE PETER. *Outline of Cultural Materials.* Human Relation Area Files, 1961.

OH, MARK E. "Cultural Pluralism and Multiethnic Congregation as a Ministry Model in an Urban Society." Pasadena, Calif.: D.Min. diss., Fuller Theological Seminary, 1988.

OSBORNE, CECIL. *The Art of Understanding Yourself.* Grand Rapids: Zondervan Publishing Houe, 1967.

SCHERMERHORN, R. A. *Comparative Ethnic Relations.* Chicago: University of Chicago Press, 1979.

SMITH, ELISE C., and LUCE, LOUISE FIBER. *Toward Internationalism: Readings in Cross-cultural Communication.* Rowley, Mass.: Newbury House Publishers, 1969.

STARK, WERNER. *Social Theory and Christian Thought.* London: Routledge and Kegan Paul, 1959.

STOTT, JOHN R. W. *One People.* Old Tappan, N.J.: Fleming H. Revell, 1982.

SWINDOLL, CHARLES R. *Improving Your Serve: The Art of Unselfish Living.* Waco, Tex.: Word Books, Publisher, 1981.

TRUESDALE, ALBERT; LYONS, GEORGE; EBY, J. WESLEY; and CLARK, NANCY, eds. *A Dictionary of the Bible and Christian Doctrine in Everyday English.* Kansas City: Beacon Hill Press of Kansas City, 1986.

WHALE, JOHN S. *Christian Doctrine.* New York: Macmillan Co., 1941.